The Macmillan Spectrum
Investor's Choice Guide to
▼
Blue Chip Stocks

WILLIAM M. BUCHSBAUM

Macmillan/Spectrum
New York

Macmillan/Spectrum

A Simon and Schuster Macmillan Company

1633 Broadway

New York, NY 10019

Library Congress Catalog Card Number: 97-071158

ISBN: 0-02861-494-1

Manufactured in the United States of America

99 98 97   9 8 7 6 5 4 3 2 1

Book Design: A&D Howell Design

Cover Design: Kevin Hanek

To my wife, Jane; my children, Tony and Ellen, Regie and Jeff, Allison and Ivan; and grandchildren, Brian, Jonathan, Jeremy, and Josseline.

CONTENTS

▼

FOREWORD

▼

I've heard people say that investing in blue chip stock is dull. Where's the sizzle? If I wanted a conservative investment, I'd buy bonds!

You want sizzle? Toss this on the fire: The 500 largest companies in America that make up the Standard & Poor's 500 Index (S&P 500) have returned a 10.7% average annual return since 1925, including the Great Depression years. In fact, take the Depression out of the equation and the return jumps to 15%. Then there are the Dow Jones Industrial Stocks whose largest dividend-paying stocks averaged 17.7% from 1978 to 1995. Even the lowest priced boring giants grew at a 20.9% clip during that same period! Is that enough sizzle for you?

These are seriously impressive returns, particularly when you consider that the risks involved are substantially less than other stock investment vehicles. This book shows you how to beat those returns in—you guessed it—blue chip stocks.

ACKNOWLEDGMENTS

▼

In a way, this book has been in the making for more than 27 years—the time I've been an active participant in the stock market. It has been a truly collaborative effort between myself and all the analysts, traders, investment advisors, professional money managers, and investors I've had the pleasure of working with through the years.

I especially would like to recognize the efforts of E. Reno Cross, without whom this book would have remained only an idea. His tireless efforts have brought together many of the concepts and strategies I've developed as an investment advisor, serving my present clients as well as any future clients who read this book and need financial advice.

Also, many thanks to my son, Tony, who as usual, did revisions like the professional that I know he is. My appreciation also goes to Laurie Harper, my agent, who has continually done all she can to bring this book to a higher level.

Bill Buchsbaum
Sante Fe, New Mexico
Summer 1997
(505) 989-2748

INTRODUCTION

▼

The term *blue chip* claims its heritage from the parlance of America's gambling halls. Originally, the blue chip was the highest denomination of casino currency (followed by red and white), which made it the preferred coinage of the seasoned gambler. Many people have compared Wall Street and the stock market with gambling. As early as 1904, Wall Streeters have used the term blue chip to describe the high-priced, dividend-producing stocks of reputable companies. Even today, the term blue chip is used most often when referring to stocks, albeit the most secure and often the largest, most well-known stocks.

Blue chip stocks often are coveted by long-term growth investors, even though those stocks vary widely in their composition, markets, and performance. From multinational General Electric to media giant Disney, all blue chip companies share some basic characteristics that make them appealing to investors:

- ▶ A long record of profit and dividend growth
- ▶ Sufficient strength to withstand economic or industry-specific downturns
- ▶ Significant and broad institutional and individual ownership

Do all blue chips make excellent investments? No. For example, RCA was a famous prudent corporation that anyone would have recommended to his grandmother as an investment. RCA's revenues came from TVs, radios, small appliances, broadcasting, publishing, and real estate, to name a few. In 1985, General Electric bought out RCA for $66.50 per share, which was about the same price the stock sold for in 1967 and just 74% above its 1929 high of $38.25 (adjusted for splits). That's an annualized return of 1% per year for 57 years. In my opinion, that's not much of a return.

And what about the famous Dow Jones blue chips? The original list, compiled by Mr. Charles H. Jones, included the most actively traded stocks, including nine railroads, Pacific Steamship, Western Union, and such luminaries as American Cotton Oil, Distilling and Cattle Feeding, Laclede Gas, and U.S. Leather Preferred, which are now gone from the list. On May 26, 1896, the first purely industrial average was published; it was composed of 12 stocks:

- ► American Cotton Oil

- ► American Sugar

- ► American Tobacco

- ► Chicago Gas

- ► Distilling and Cattle Feeding

- ► General Electric

- ► Laclede Gas

- ► National Lead

- ► North American Company

- ► Tennessee Coal and Iron

- ► U.S. Leather Preferred

- ► U.S. Rubber

Baldwin Locomotive was on the list in 1916, but was off by 1924. In 1925, the list included Paramount Famous Laskey and Remington Typewriters; both were off the list by 1927. In 1928, the Dow Jones Industrial Average expanded from 20 to 30 stocks, with such common household names as Nash Motors, Postum, Wright Aeronautical, and Victor Talking Machines (which was off the list by 1969 due to a merger with RCA—and we already know what a good investment that was). In 1950, Corn Products Refining made the list. Nine years later, it was replaced by Swift and Company. These were all well-established blue chip companies, but if you had invested in those companies then, you would have lost a great deal of money.

Fast forward to the 1970s. Between 1972 and 1974, investors in Bristol-Myers saw their stock fall from $9 per share to $4; Teledyne fell from $11 to $3; and McDonald's, currently in the Dow Jones, plummeted from $15 to $3. These are not insignificant companies; they are all dividend paying, national brand entities.

How do you sort through today's blue chips (there are more than 500 companies) and decide which ones to invest in and which ones to avoid? The 30 largest—those included in the Dow Jones Industrial Average—account for about one trillion dollars of assets. To pick the winners seems almost daunting. Due to an explosion in sheer numbers and kinds of investments readily available to the average investor, the task seems impossible and that doesn't include the many more company stocks, mutual funds, and real estate.

Keep Focused with a Goal or Dream

What is your financial goal? To pay for the finest college or graduate school for your children? To own your own business? To have a retirement of deserved ease and fullness? To be free from financial worries? To accumulate enough excess wealth to make generous gifts to your favorite charities? Whatever your goal, you won't achieve it just because you're nice; it will require careful planning and implementation through informed and careful investing.

To some, investing is a hobby: They love the process of selecting different kinds of investments, following their progress, and changing them as needed. But to most, investing is a means to an end, a way to accomplish a financial goal. Whether you're an avid money manager or a passive investor, you must have at least a basic knowledge of successful investment techniques to stay on course and to keep out of trouble. This book will provide this basic knowledge.

Choices, Changes, and Challenges

Consider this: In 1950, there were fewer than 100 mutual funds selling shares to the public, and blue chips constituted most of their portfolio. Today, investors have more than 8,500 stock and bond mutual funds to choose from—which is more than the common stock choices available on the New York Stock Exchange and the American Stock Exchange combined.

Another major change in the investment climate is the pace of the change itself. For example, the fortunes of even the most solid companies can shift fundamentally in a short period of time. And rapid technological changes have shortened the life cycles of many high-tech products, making yesterday's state-of-the-art tomorrow's basement bargain.

Other challenges come from the globalization of business. While our shrinking world adds new investment opportunities, it also means tougher competition. And, of course, there are the risks of changes in currency valuation, international trade laws, government regulations, and so on.

The unfortunate fact is that more often than not, what looks like a significant development really isn't, and what looks like trivial activity can truly move markets. The smart investor is not a manic financial whiz frantically chasing daily headlines. Rather, the recipe for competent and profitable investing is one part patience and one part informed calmness. When it comes to fad, fashion, and emotion, take three heaping doses of skepticism.

Probably the most important thing to remember is that smart investing does not involve lots of transactions, such as calling your broker every day, selling short, trading actively, switching mutual funds frequently, or using exotic hedging techniques. Actually, this kind of approach is counterproductive and often leads to ruin. The smart investors, regardless of income, occupation, and investment experience, are the ones who calmly make a plan, select the right investments, and give the plan lots of time to work.

In this book, I explain the general topics of investing, risk, how to analyze, how to choose appropriate investments, and how to find the bluest of blue chips. I show you how to analyze a candidate quickly and effectively; how and when to use margin; how to use other techniques to structure your investment portfolio; and how to know when to sell. I also discuss the broader stock market; a few important economic and demographic factors; interest rates and what they mean to your portfolio; and some common investors' mistakes and how to avoid them.

This book is not designed to fully educate you on the subtleties of the stock market and its participants, nor does it give you an MBA or a degree in economics. This book provides you with a methodology to make money in the stock market by investing in blue chip companies.

CASE STUDY

Let's look at an actual real life investment situation, with real goals and real outcomes. A client of mine, let's call him John, came to me with $329,000 in 1991. His portfolio consisted of General Electric, Bristol Myers, Exxon, Chevron, DuPont and Phillip Morris. In the five years I have managed his account (which is a trust established for children in their 30s), the portfolio has performed excellently. Using the same techniques I have outlined in this book, the account grew to over $1 million by December, 1996. And that included withdrawals of close to $100,000.

The returns on this account have outpaced the objectives set forth earlier in this book (that is, a 12%-15% compounded annual rate of return), mainly due to economic trends, moderating inflation and interest rates, and higher corporate earnings—not to mention the baby boomers, who have played such an important part in the market cycle and will continue to do so. But remember, the core investments were sound and were chosen using the system outlined in Chapter 5. I look for continued stock appreciation in this account for years to come.

LET'S REMEMBER THIS:

- ▶ The best blue chip stocks have long records of profit, have dividend growth, and can withstand bad economic times.

- ▶ While the Dow Jones Industrial Average includes 30 of some of the largest companies in the world, these companies are not necessarily the only blue chips to consider.

- ▶ The number of investment vehicles has grown dramatically, which makes the process of choosing stock more difficult.

CHAPTER 1

▼

PLAYING TO WIN

WHAT WE ARE GOING TO TALK ABOUT IN THIS CHAPTER:

- ▶ The Basics of Investing
- ▶ The Best Ways to Define Your Goals
- ▶ How to Create a Plan to Achieve Your Goals

WHAT IS INVESTING?

Investing is simply deferring consumption. That is to say, investors are actively choosing to not spend their money on goods and services now; rather, they are setting the money aside to purchase goods and services sometime in the future.

Whether or not you're investing in blue chip stocks, there are two simple truths about investing. First, investing entails risk. There are two kinds of risk: volatility and inflation. (I will discuss both in detail in the next chapter.) Your success depends on your ability to reduce risk without passing up reasonable rewards. And reasonable rewards, over time, are possibly enough to generate the wealth you want.

I will show you how to minimize your risk without sacrificing reasonable rewards. If you're in a hurry to cash in or to make a killing, this book is not for you. Instead, you should buy a lottery ticket or enter a publisher's sweepstakes, because that way, all you risk is the price of the ticket or the cost of magazine subscriptions.

The second truth is that the best opportunities for building wealth occur in healthy, growing companies. Therefore, your prosperity depends on the world's prosperity—not just America, but the world.

Money Talks: To make money, you must have a plan and you must be patient. If you're patient, the economic climate in the years ahead coupled with a nearly inexhaustible number of ways to invest in the world economy can make the next decade or so very profitable for you.

DEFINE YOUR GOALS

You must first decide what your investment goals are. Do you want to retire, build a new house, buy a fancy car, ensure an education for your children or grandchildren? Setting goals is very personal: Your own style and preferences will guide you. However, if you set nebulous, generalized goals, such as "financial security" or "a comfortable retirement," you'll have trouble measuring your progress. You may even struggle to maintain interest. Vaguely defined investment goals can lead to halfhearted efforts to achieve them.

Many investors do not have specific investment goals. Would you build a house without a plan? Or plan not to finish it? Would you leave for a two-week vacation without making arrangements for lodging or transportation? Perhaps you would if you value spontaneity. But your investment goals and financial future should be anything but spontaneous.

Set goals you can hold onto—goals that excite you. Instead of "financial security," why not a million dollars net worth by age 60? Instead of "a comfortable retirement," why not a two bedroom condo on a golf course on Maui, plus an investment portfolio that will yield $3,000 a month to supplement your pension? Now *those* are goals.

WHY DO YOU NEED GOALS?

Whatever your goals may be, it is essential to have them. Why do you need goals? If you don't have a goal, you won't know if you reach it! If you have reasonable financial goals, you *can* achieve them. Keeping your goals fixed in your mind disciplines yourself along the way. How else will you know whether the advice you receive from books or from your broker is of any value? And how will you know when to eliminate investments that are not meeting your expectations?

Make Your Goals Count!

Establishing goals also is important because different goals require different investment plans. You must decide what your goals are and choose which ones are very important and which ones are less important. Your job is to quantify your goals, qualify them, reconcile the differing outcomes, and prioritize your goals—all in a way that can be translated into an effective investment plan. It's not an easy job, but you can do it.

Dollars & $ense: The only way to prioritize your goals is to quantify them. So write them down on paper, and number them from the most important to the least important, or from the most urgent to the least urgent.

For example, say you want to replace your old car with a new one in two to three years. As soon as you narrow down the type of car you want, you've quantified that goal. Seems simple enough. Say you also want to fund a college education account for your son or daughter. That, too, is relatively easy to quantify: In about 18 years from now you'll need $100,000 for the average four-year state institution (that is, if your child wants to attend an average college). But here's the rub: Which one do you fund first? If your investment dollars are limited, like most people's, you probably can't fully save for both goals. Your child's education is extremely important, but your car is on its last leg. As you can see, qualifying your investment goals can quickly get difficult.

Dollars & $ense: In 18 years, the cost of tuition for the average four-year college in today's dollars will be more than $100,000. The only way to effectively plan for this expense is to start early.

Devise a Plan to Achieve Your Goals

To achieve your goals, you should devise a plan regardless of your current style of savings and investing. For example, if you tend to neglect your finances, you should create a plan with neglect in mind. Many successful investors put their portfolios on autopilot, spending only a few hours each year monitoring their performance; others prefer to pay close attention to what's happening. Whatever kind of investor you are, you can accumulate remarkable sums of money by applying the techniques outlined in later chapters.

Your reasons for investing may be different than mine (for example, you might be saving for the care of an elderly parent, whereas I might be focusing exclusively on my retirement), but our expectations of those investments are probably the same. Ultimately, we both want to reach those goals and we both need a plan to attain them.

The single most important thing you can do to achieve a successful investment program is to develop an investment plan. You don't need to write a 20-page technical journal; instead, you need to answer three questions:

1. What do you want?

2. How long do you have to get what you want?

3. How much money could you lose and still feel comfortable with your financial situation?

Once you've considered these important questions, the following sections will help you answer them and build a strong investment plan.

BUILDING YOUR INVESTMENT PLAN

Here's a simple and effective way to get started. Draw a vertical line down the center of a piece of paper. On the left, list your assets—everything you own that's worth any money. List each item at its current market value, not what you wish it was worth. On the right, list your liabilities—all the money you owe on your assets, as well as any money you owe that is not related to those assets. Then total each column vertically and subtract your total liabilities from your total assets to get your net worth. Table 1-1 shows an example. (Note: Your net worth is total assets less total liabilities.)

Table 1-1   Personal Balance Sheet

Assets		Liabilities	
Cash	$14,000	Mortgage	$80,000
House Market Value	150,000	Student Loan	3,500
Stocks	10,000	Car Loan	6,000
Personal Assets	5,000	Credit Card Balance	1,000
Totals	$179,000		$90,500
		Net Worth	**$88,500**

Now that you know where you are, you're probably thinking about where you want to be. Before you get there, you have to start making investing a habit. About that goal: Don't devise the most ingenious investment plan ever conceived, but create one that suits you—a plan you can stick with.

THE INVESTING HABIT

If you have millions to invest, you can take a short vacation from this section. If you're starting with a small amount to invest, the best way to acquire measurable wealth is to develop the habit of adding something to the pot on a regular basis and putting the money where it can do the most good for you.

The investing habit can really pay off. For example, if you put $5,000 in a bank, it will earn a nice, safe ±4% interest. Twenty years later, when you claim your deposit (assuming the bank is still there), you discover that it's grown to a not-so-impressive $11,000 plus change.

 Dollars & Sense: Remember to pay yourself first. Write a check every month to your investment plan first, then pay the rest of your bills.

Here's another example: A friend puts $5,000 in a one-year certificate of deposit (CD) at the same bank, with instructions to roll over the proceeds into a new CD every 12 months. In addition, every month he buys another CD for $100 and issues the same instructions. Over 20 years, he earns an average of 6% interest. By rolling his CDs over at each maturity, he captures a higher interest rate on average because maturities on the new CDs were progressively longer. After 20 years, his nest egg has grown to nearly $63,000.

That's a lot better, but it still isn't a lot of money by today's standards, nor quite possibly the investment you want. Investing in blue chip stocks has been one of the best vehicles for growth over the long-term.

Suppose your goal is much loftier—you want to have a nest egg of half a million dollars. You have 20 years to get there and $5,000 to start with. You're willing to investigate alternatives that should boost your return above what you would earn in a bank account. What's a reasonable return to plan on, and how much will you have to contribute along the way?

For reasons you'll learn about in later chapters, an average annual return of 12% to 15% over the long-run is a reasonable expectation for individuals using the techniques described in this book. At 15%, with $5,000 to start with, you'll reach your $500,000 goal by contributing $320 a month to your investment account. With a 12% return, $450 a month will get you there in 20 years.

Less ambitious plans can also work wonders. Starting from zero, putting $50 a month into an investment that pays a compounded average annual total return of 15% for 20 years will get you a nest egg of more than $75,000. Stick to the plan for 30 years and you'll have more than $350,000. Double your contribution and you'll double the size of your nest egg.

Starting small and gradually increasing your monthly investment amount as your income grows is another option. For example, you can begin by putting $100 a month into your investment account for five years, raise it to $200 a month for the next five years, $300 a month for years 11 through 15, and $400 a month for years 16 through 20. At the end of 20 years, you'll have nearly $227,000. Boost your monthly amount to $500 for years 21 through 25 and your fund will grow to almost $500,000, assuming you can earn an average of 15% per year.

Time, not timing, is the important ingredient in a successful investment program. Getting started early gives your investment and earnings more time to grow.

PUT TIME ON YOUR SIDE

Take a look at Table 1-2. Two sisters, Mary and Jane, are both considering funding their retirement accounts. Mary invests $10,000 in a long-term investment at the age of 40 and leaves it alone.

Jane decides to wait and begins making $5,000 annual investments into a similar investment for the next seven years. Assume that both sisters earn 10% per year on their investments. As you can see, Mary has invested $10,000 and Jane has invested $40,000 towards their retirement. Surprisingly, Mary, who made only one investment, ends up with substantially more money than Jane. The reason: time.

| | Table 1-2 Mary and Jane | |
| | Retirement Plan Funding Schedule | |
Age	Mary	Jane
40	$10,000	
55		$5,000
56		5,000

continues

Age	Mary	Jane
57		5,000
58		5,000
59		5,000
60		5,000
61		5,000
62		5,000
Value at 65	$108,347	$76,105

How common is an average annual return of 15%? For the 10-year period ending in mid-1995, at least 99 mutual funds delivered 15% or more, about 350 mutual funds achieved a 12% or better annual return. As for stocks, the Dow Jones Industrial Average (the Dow) tripled during the 1980s—a remarkable performance, though not unique. In the 10-year period from 1942 to 1952, and in the one from 1953 to 1963, the Dow tripled. Take a look at Figure 1-1. Each bar represents the value of $1 invested in each

Figure 1-1   Performance History of Various Investments and Inflation 1960-1994

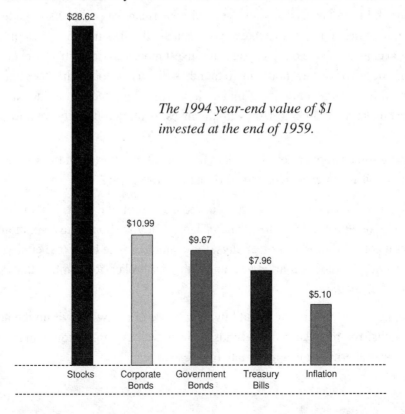

The 1994 year-end value of $1 invested at the end of 1959.

different investment at the end of 1959. By the end of 1994, 25 years later, stocks returned $28.62 on that original $1 investment! One dollar invested in 1959 in corporate bonds returned $10.99, while $1 invested in safer government bonds returned only $9.67 during the same period. Worse yet, $1 invested in Treasury bills grew to $7.96 in 35 years. Inflation during the same period cost investors $5.10 of their investment. For the rest of the 1990s, a mediocre market would be enough for the Dow to end the decade in the neighborhood of 8,000 to 10,000. But helping you achieve mediocre investment results isn't the goal of this book. If you follow my investment structure, you should do better than mediocre. Much better.

These examples are oversimplified; they don't take into account taxes or commission. The point is the same, however. Making a habit of investing is an important key to making investing a success.

Play the Winning Game

If you thought devising a plan was hard, wait 'til you try this. There are no right or wrong investments goals. Goals can be whatever you want them to be, but make them attainable and realistic. Your goals will be influenced by your income, your job security, your ability to take risks, your age, and your financial prospects in general. In addition, the time you have to achieve your goals will influence the kinds of investments you consider. For example, you can't invest money in stocks if you're counting on that money to buy a new house in 10 months—the risk is too high! Does that mean you should leave large amounts of money in your savings account at the bank? No. You must match your time horizon with the investment, if you really want to be successful.

Here are some simple rules about time horizons. Let's start with the shortest time horizon, that is the unexpected, and work out to retirement:

▶ You have to plan for the unexpected: the leaky roof, the valve job on the Volvo, or a broken leg. Most experts agree that you should have six months of net income in some sort of savings, for example, in the bank or, better yet, in a very liquid money market account with your broker. Remember, that's *net* income, not *gross*.

▶ Suppose you're thinking about buying a house or a new car within the next 24 months. You must keep those funds aside as well. Again, a money market fund or other alternative is appropriate for these monies.

▶ You must also fund (invest) or be in the process of funding your retirement plan. I recommend you fund the maximum available to you into your 401(k), IRA, or other pre-tax retirement plan before you seriously consider additional investment in stocks or other vehicles.

▶ Finally, after you've taken care of all of the preceding, any left-over money is what I call true investment dollars.

Money Talks: Most people spend more time planning their vacation than they do planning their retirement!

For those who can regularly set aside money for investments, see Table 1-3, which plainly exhibits the power of planning.

Table 1-3	The Value of Regular Investing				
Monthly Investment	**5 Years**	**10 Years**	**15 Years**	**20 Years**	**25 Years**
$50	$3,698	$9,208	$17,416	$29,646	$47,866
100	7,396	18,415	34,832	59,291	95,732
250	18,489	46,038	87,080	148,229	239,329
500	36,978	92,075	174,162	296,457	478,659

Table assumes an annual investment return of 8%, compounded monthly, but does not reflect taxes.

For money to be true investment money, you must be able to live without it for at least five years—the length of a full market cycle. Many investors come to me and talk about their goal of making their available funds work harder for them, and they're very excited about stocks and the promise of much higher returns than their money market accounts are paying. Often, their last sentence is "But I must have access to the money; I just might need it to buy a new car."

There's a fundamental difference between investment money and "I might need it" money. Again, you *must* match your investments with an appropriate time horizon, or you will not be successful. It's just that simple.

Let's Remember This:

- ▶ Put time on your side. Invest for the long-term.

- ▶ To build wealth, buy stock in growing companies.

- ▶ Set goals that are specific and stick with those goals.

▼

The Two Faces of Risk

What We Are Going to Talk About in This Chapter:

> ▶ What is Risk?
>
> ▶ How Inflation Affects Your Investments
>
> ▶ How Volatility Affects Your Investments

The Two Faces of Risk

To answer the question of how much risk you can take effectively, you must first understand what risk is. Most people think risk is the chance you take of losing all or part of the money you put into an investment. That's true, basically—but it goes further.

For any investor, there are only two kinds of risk: inflation and volatility.

Money Talks:

Remember there are no investments that are completely free from risk.

INFLATION RISK

You can always invest in such vehicles as savings accounts in federally insured banks, savings and loans, and credit unions, which virtually guarantee that you'll get all your money back plus the interest you were promised. Despite the problems a few years ago of some institutions and the fund that insured their deposits, some choices are safe. But you have risk with these investments, even government-guaranteed investments. You run the risk that your return will be less than the rate of inflation. Indeed, because of their close relationship to the rate of inflation, savings accounts, CDs, Treasury bills, savings bonds, and other government-backed investments establish a useful benchmark for measuring risk.

So, how do you define inflation risk? *Inflation risk* is the chance you take that you will earn less from an investment than the rate of inflation or less than the interest available at the time from insured savings certificates or U. S. Treasury-backed obligations. If you can't expect to do better than 4% or 5% on your money, there seems to be little reason to take the risk of losing almost all of your interest on that investment due to inflation.

Inflation is the gradual loss of purchasing power due to the general increase in the prices of goods and services. What you could buy five years ago for $1.00 may now cost $1.27. The effect this has on you is simple: If your investments are not producing enough return to outpace inflation, then you're better off not making the investment.

Table 2-1 dramatizes the effects of inflation and how it can wreak havoc with your life. For example, postage stamps increased from $.15 in 1980 to $.32 in 1995, a 113% increase! The cost of Levi jeans, coveted the world over for their durability and affordability, went from $11.02 in 1980 to $20.95 in 1995, a 90% increase. The average car in 1980 cost $7,574; today the average car costs more than $19,600—an increase of more than 160%! Has your income gone up that much since 1980?

Table 2-1 How 15 Years of Inflation Have Affected Prices			
Item	*1980*	*1995*	*Increase*
Postage Stamp	$.15	$.32	113%
Levi's 501 Jeans	$11	$21	90%
Car	$7,574	$19,660	160%

Source: U.S. Department of Commerce, Levi Strauss

The sad truth is that the $1 you had in 1980 buys less than $.50 worth of goods and services today. Inflation has caused, and will continue to cause, your purchasing power to plummet.

Economists measure inflation with the *Consumer Price Index*, or CPI (see Table 2-2). The CPI attempts to measure changes in the prices of goods and services purchased by urban consumers. (The statistics are gathered in large metropolitan areas; rural prices, therefore, are not included.) The Bureau of Labor Statistics computes the index monthly using data collected in 85 major cities from nearly 25,000 retail stores. The index reflects price changes of approximately 400 goods and services, in seven broad categories: food, clothing, housing, transportation, medical care, entertainment, and other. The base year is 1967, which set the index at 100. So, when the CPI measured 328.4 in 1986, it meant that the general level of prices, as measured by the index, had more than tripled in 29 years.

Table 2-2   The History of Inflation

Year	CPI	Year	CPI
1971	3.36%	1981	8.94%
1972	3.41	1982	3.87
1973	8.8	1983	3.8
1974	12.20	1984	3.95
1975	7.01	1985	3.77
1976	4.81	1986	1.13
1977	6.77	1987	4.41
1978	9.03	1988	4.42
1979	13.31	1989	4.65
1980	12.40	1990	6.11
Average Annual Increase			6.31%

To see the true effects of inflation, you need to look at the long-term picture. Figure 2-1 shows what inflation would do to $100,000 over a period of 5, 10, 20, and 30 years.

Figure 2-1   How Inflation Affects Purchasing Power

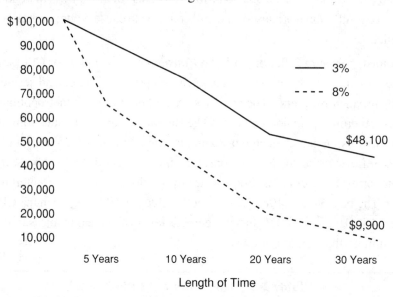

As you can see, even at a moderate rate of inflation, say 3%, $100,000 is worth only $48,100 in 30 years. If you were planning for your retirement with these funds, the prospects would be sobering, particularly when the average annual rate of inflation over the past 10 years has been closer to 6.3%.

VOLATILITY RISK

Volatility can be a serious risk for the short-term investor. But for the long-term investor, volatility can be good. Why? It's the engine that drives higher rates of return. If stocks didn't exhibit short-term fluctuations in price, investors wouldn't demand compensation and, as a result, stocks wouldn't pay more in the long-run than a money market fund or other non-volatile investments. Another way to look at the risk/return trade-off is in terms of ranges of annual returns. The riskiness of an asset can be approximated by the difference between its minimum and maximum returns. Figure 2-2 shows this relationship.

The graph in Figure 2-2 looks at ranges of annual returns for five major asset classes over the last 67 years. The top of each bar represents the highest calendar year

Figure 2-2   The Case for Long-term Investing

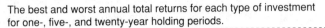

The best and worst annual total returns for each type of investment
for one-, five-, and twenty-year holding periods.

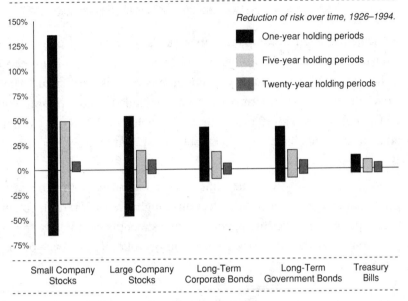

return during the period; the bottom of each bar represents the lowest calendar year return. As you can see, volatility, as expressed by the price movements of each of the investments listed, significantly decreases as you extend the time period. When you go from 2 to 3 years to 15 years, the price fluctuations in large company stocks decreases from 100% over any one-year period to less than 50% over any five-year period, to less than 18% over a 20-year period, which is about the same as long-term bonds!

Why would you, a rational person, invest your money in long-term government bonds rather than large stocks if you were going to leave the money invested for a period of 20 years? The rate of return on the stocks for that period is 12.5%; it's only 5.2% for long-term bonds for the same period. Yet the relative volatility of the two is nearly the same. Similarly, if you put your money in stocks rather than short-term treasuries for less than five years, you exposed that money to a 500% increase in risk!

Dollars & Sense: CDs are loans you make to the bank, just as bonds are loans you make to corporations or the government. The return of CDs has been substantially lower over time than stocks and the interest you earn on them is usually taxable.

It is evident that even a comparatively risky asset, such as common stocks, becomes relatively safe over long time periods. Over a 10-year holding period, for example, the chance of losing money in common stocks is very small. The worst outcome over the last 67 years was a –0.9% compounded annual return, which included the Great Depression (refer to Figure 2-2). Table 2-3 shows that as your holding period increases, the chances of your stock investment going down dramatically decreases.

You're probably familiar with the phrase "no pain, no gain." In the context of investing, "no pain, no gain" means that to realize higher rates of return, you must be willing to accept greater price fluctuation. No investment is completely free of risk; however, deciding whether that risk is inflation or volatility is how you begin to develop your strategy.

Table 2-3 1960-1994		
Holding Period	*S & P 500*	
	Up	*Down*
1 Year	27	8
5 Years	29	2
10 Years	26	0
15 Years	21	0

In Table 2-3, you can see that on a short-term basis, stocks are riskier (as measured by the Standard & Poor's 500 Index); as your time horizon increases, however, the risk gets much lower. For example, in a one-year holding period, stocks lost ground eight times from 1960 to 1994. As soon as you get to a 10-year holding period or longer, stock levels never went down! Because investing in blue chip stocks by its very nature is long-term, turn your attention to the advantages of volatility, how to manage it, and how to defeat the real risk of inflation.

CASE STUDY

In 1987, an oil executive came to me prior to his retirement from Chevron. We mapped out a plan of attack to give him a fixed monthly income from his $700,000, which was the result of rolling over his lump-sum distribution from Chevron. All the funds were invested in fixed-income securities (bonds or equivalents) to slowly generate a steady income. Three years later, the account had grown to $740,000, in spite of the monthly withdrawals. Because of the effects of inflation over time, my client was finally convinced that we should add some growth to the portfolio. So we invested $200,000 in blue chip stocks. With subsequent withdrawals of more than $250,000, the stock account is worth $1,300,000, which of course now creates a tax problem for him due to the appreciation. Everyone should have such a problem! You never go broke taking a profit, and you never go broke paying taxes on the profits—as long as you don't spend the tax part of the profits.

LET'S REMEMBER THIS:

▶ Investors face only two kinds of risk: inflation and volatility.

▶ Volatility is the engine that drives higher returns.

▶ Blue chip stocks have generated a compounded annual total return of 10.7% from 1929 through 1996, which includes the Great Depression.

▼

DIVIDE AND CONQUER

WHAT WE ARE GOING TO TALK ABOUT IN THIS CHAPTER:

- ► What is Diversification?
- ► How Does Diversification Effect Risk and Return?
- ► How Can Diversifying Benefit You?

DIVERSIFICATION

Although I will show you how to reduce your risks when buying blue chip stocks, first you should understand the concept of diversification to be able to maximize your investment returns. One proven method to reduce your risk as an investor is to diversify your holdings. This doesn't mean you must acquire 50 or 100 different stocks (it is possible to overdiversify). Diversification depends not only on the number of stocks an investor owns, but also on the types of stocks chosen. If you own 10 stocks in the utility industry, your portfolio is not diversified; these stocks will likely move together in response to changes in interest rates. Even a portfolio of stocks in the airline, auto, and steel industries will be strongly influenced by changes in the business cycle and, therefore, does not constitute diversification.

Investment risks are related to different economic variables, such as consumer spending, business investment, interest rates, and other factors, not to mention irrational investor behavior. Therefore, it is more prudent to select stocks that don't follow the same pattern in response to changes in economic variables.

PROPER DIVERSIFICATION

There are at least three good reasons to diversify your investment:

1. It's common sense: You shouldn't put all your eggs in one basket.

2. No investment performs well all the time; usually, when something declines, something else rises.

3. Most investment experts believe that you can actually increase your return with a sensible strategy of diversification. Most studies indicate that a portfolio of eight to ten stocks in different industries exposed to different risks will tend to substantially reduce the overall risk.

Table 3-1 gives you a numerical comparison of the ups and downs of various investment markets. This is a snapshot of recent years, plus inflation figures. The investment figures are total returns, which means they include price changes and assume that all earnings from the investments, if any, are reinvested.

Table 3-1	Assets Perform Differently at Different Times				
	1975	*1979*	*1985*	*1990*	*1994*
Inflation Rate	6.9%	13.3%	3.8%	6.1%	2.7%
Dow Jones Industrials	44.8%	10.6%	33.6%	–0.6%	5.0%
Lehman Brothers Long-term Treasury Bills	8.3%	–0.5%	31.6%	6.4%	–7.6%
Donoghue's Money Market Index	N/A	12.8%	7.2%	7.8%	3.8%
Gold	–24.9%	12.6%	6.9%	–2.7%	–2.4%
Real Estate Investment Trusts	27.3%	19.3%	0.8%	–43.6%	0.8%

The inflation rate shows an increase from 6.9% in 1975 to 13.3% in 1979, dropping to 3.8% in 1985, only to rise again to 6.1% in 1990, followed by a drop to 2.7% in 1994. During that same period, the Dow increased 44.8% in 1975, 10.6% in 1979,

33.6% in 1985, lost .6% in 1990, and gained 5% in 1994. Long-term Treasury bonds gained 8.3% in 1975, lost .5% in 1979, increased 31.6% in 1985 and 6.4% in 1990, and then lost 7.6% in 1994. The money market index did not exist in 1975, but it returned 12.8% in 1979, 7.2% in 1985, 7.8% in 1990, and yielded 3.8% in 1994.

Gold tends to react in unison with the rate of inflation. As inflation dissipated in 1975 to 6.9%, gold dropped 24.9%; when inflation rose 13.3% in 1979, gold more than doubled to 12.6% (higher during the so-called run to safety). Gold only increased 6.9% in 1985 as inflation subsided to 3.8%. A drop in gold in 1990 of 2.7% and in 1994 of 2.4% mirrored a continued drop in the rate of inflation.

 Money Talks: Investments such as gold and real estate tend to be inflation-sensitive; consequently, when stocks are down, these assets tend to be up. That's the power of diversification.

Of course, a different selection of years would have shown a different pattern. For example, even with dividends included, the Dow turned in dismal performances in 1973, 1974, and 1977. Gold soared in each of those years and again in 1993, while real estate investment trusts fell so sharply in 1973 and 1974 that their survival as an investment vehicle was in serious doubt. They climbed strongly in 1991, 1992, and 1993.

Invest in whatever you want, but invest in vehicles that do not move in unison. Diversify your holdings.

Figure 3-1 demonstrates the concept of portfolio diversification. The graph on the left shows how the value of stocks increased and decreased over time. Note the significant falloff in value in the shaded region.

The middle graph shows how the value of bonds increased and decreased over the same time period. Note that bonds went up significantly during the period stocks didn't.

The graph on the right shows how a portfolio consisting of half stocks and half bonds would have performed in the same time period. Stability is evident, due to the benefits of diversification.

Figure 3-1   Benefits of Diversification

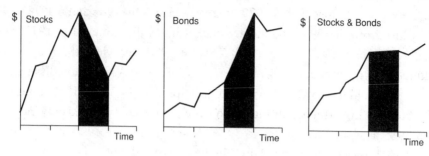

By Diversifying, a deep loss in one asset class...   ...may be offset by gains in another.   The net result is a more stable portfolio of investments.

Diversification applies to both asset classes and individual securities. An *asset class* is a group of investments that are similar in performance to each other and dissimilar to other groups. Up to a point, risk in a portfolio can be reduced by adding additional asset classes or by adding additional securities to an existing asset class.

Because it is improbable to pick only winning stocks every time, the smart investor must find ways to compensate for mistakes, miscalculations, or just bad luck—there will always be one of these. It's a good idea to make sure that no single stock represents more than 5% to 10% of your portfolio. Naturally, if you have only a small amount to invest, it will be more difficult to properly diversify. Regardless of the amount of money you have to invest, however, you must concentrate on companies with the best potential. If you can be a winner with two out of three stocks, or four out of seven stocks, you will increase your chances of making a great deal of money.

Figure 3-2 shows the benefits of diversification and the power it has as an investment strategy.

The two bars on the left illustrate what would happen over 25 years if you invested $100,000 in an 8% fixed-rate instrument, such as a government bond. As you can see, your $100,000 grows to $684,850.

The two bars on the right illustrate what would happen if you invested that same $100,000 in five different investment vehicles over the same 25-year period, assuming you invested the money as follows:

▶ Your first investment of $20,000 went straight to zero. You broke even on the second $20,000. So far, this is a zero return. (In fact, you have lost $20,000.)

▶ You got a 5% return on the third $20,000, a 10% return on the fourth $20,000, and a 15% return on the fifth $20,000.

Figure 3-2   Power of Diversification Graph

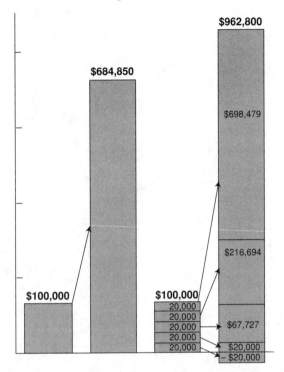

As you can see, even with widely diverse performance, the diversified portfolio grew to $962,800, which is 40% higher, or a full $277,950 more than the first example. Diversify.

Let's Remember This:

- ▶ Diversify your investment portfolio; proper diversification is critical to successful investing.

- ▶ Benefits of diversification are increased performance and decreased portfolio risk.

- ▶ Under-diversification limits returns; over-diversification also limits returns.

▼

What Color is Your Stock?

What We Are Going to Talk About in This Chapter:

- ▶ Definitions of Stocks and Blue Chip Stocks
- ▶ What Are the Different Stock Exchanges?
- ▶ The Value of Historical Stock Performance

What is the Difference Between Stocks and Blue Chip Stocks?

Before explaining what a blue chip stock is, it's important for you to understand what a stock is. When investors talk about stocks, they usually mean common stocks. A share of *common stock* represents a share of ownership in the company that issues it; it ties the investor's fortunes to those of the company. And because business by its very nature is risky, owning part of a business is equally risky. The price of the stock rises and falls with the company's performance and how investors think the company will perform in the future. If the company pays a dividend, it usually comes from profits; if profits fall, a dividend payment may be cut or eliminated.

Blue chip stocks are shares of common stock in nationally known companies that have a long history of profit growth and dividend payments. Some examples of blue chip stocks include Coca Cola, General Electric, Gillette, and Du Pont. Blue chip stocks tend to be relatively high-priced and pay a low dividend relative to their price. Investors are willing to pay more for the lower risk associated with owning these stocks. These companies are frequently involved in multiple industries or in different segments of the same industry. They tend to be massive by any standard and employ thousands, and even tens of thousands. Some are very capital intensive, while others are more labor dependent.

A blue chip stock should have billions in assets, and should have sales in more than one country. A blue chip stock usually has at least 250 million shares or more of common stock outstanding and its stock must be traded on one of the national exchanges (New York Stock Exchange, the American Stock Exchange, or NASDAQ). Finally, to be a blue chip, a company's stock must have been traded publicly for at least 15 years.

THE MARKETS

What are the markets? Most investors hear daily that the market was "up 50 points" or "down 40 points." But what is the market?

Actually, there are hundreds of markets. The two most commonly referred to are the Dow (Dow Jones Industrial Average) and the Standard & Poor's 500 (S & P 500). Let's look at these two markets more closely, as they are the ones most commonly used by blue chip investors.

CHOOSING A COMMON STOCK

Regardless of the exchange it's traded on, the secret to choosing a good common stock is really no secret at all. The winning techniques you will learn about in Chapter 6 are proven to be effective. The way you assemble and apply those techniques is what will make the difference. They won't work all the time—nothing does. But if you apply them as outlined, they will work successfully and consistently enough to make you wealthier than you are now.

Having the right information about a company and knowing how to interpret that information is more important than any other factors that receive credit for the success of the latest market

continues

genius. Information is even more important than timing, because when you find a company that looks promising, you can't relax. Good stocks tend to stay good, so you can take the time to investigate before you invest.

You get the information you need to size up a company's prospect in many places, and a lot of it is free. In Chapter 9, you will find a complete discussion of where to find this information.

But for now, if it's wealth you want, look to the stock market. No matter what kinds of stocks you buy or which exchanges you use, stocks are the best investment vehicle around. No other investment delivers as well as stocks over the long-run to intelligent people with average resources, average willingness to take risks, and limited time to spend on active management. Not real estate. Not gold. Not bonds. And certainly not savings accounts. Stocks aren't the only things that belong in your investment portfolio, but they are the most important.

THE DOW JONES INDUSTRIAL AVERAGE (THE DOW)

Many investors associate blue chip stocks with the Dow Jones Industrial Average (hereafter, simply referred to as the Dow), which is the well-known market index of 30 industrial companies listed on the New York Stock Exchange.

The Dow (where most stocks are so-called blue chip) is the most widely followed stock market average. When the market trend is described, this is the index usually referred to. It was first calculated in 1884 by Charles Dow, who averaged the prices of 11 important stocks. The average was broadened in 1928 to include 30 stocks. Since then, companies have been added or dropped. Currently, the 30 corporations represented in the index are large, blue chip companies. The divisor has been changed frequently to compensate for stock splits, stock dividends, and other factors, and is no longer equal to the number of stocks in the index.

Although the Dow continues to be the most publicized index, there are now Dow Jones Indexes for 20 transportation company stocks, 15 utility company stocks, and a composite index of the 65 stocks in all three indexes. The names of the blue chip stocks included in each index are printed each Monday in the *Wall Street Journal*.

The Dow stock averages are price-weighted; that is, the component stock prices are added together and the sum is divided by another figure (the divisor). As a result, a high-priced stock has a greater effect on the index than a low-priced stock. Over the long term, the Dow has been an effective indicator of the direction of the overall market.

STANDARD AND POOR'S 500 INDEX (S&P 500)

In addition to the Dow, the Standard and Poor Corporation (S&P) compiles indexes that are widely used by investors. The S&P 500 Index, also known as the *composite index*, and the S&P 400 Index, known as the *industrial index*, are among the most important and the most followed indexes.

After the Dow, the S&P 500 is the most widely followed barometer of stock market movements. Originally, the S&P 500 was computed using only 233 stocks. In 1957, it was changed to include a sample of 500 stocks. On a daily basis, its movement is representative of the movement of the stock market as a whole thanks to its large sample size and the fact that the index is market weighted. The S&P 500 stock index is made up of 400 industrial, 20 transportation, 40 utility stocks, and 40 financial stocks. The index consists primarily of New York Stock Exchange-listed companies, but it also includes some American Stock Exchange and over-the-counter (NASDAQ) stocks.

NEW YORK STOCK EXCHANGE (NYSE) AND AMERICAN STOCK EXCHANGE (AMEX)

Common stocks are traded primarily on nine stock exchanges in the U.S. The largest is the New York Stock Exchange (NYSE), located in Manhattan's financial district, which lists more than 1,600 companies with more than 50 billion shares issued and a market value of more than $2 trillion.

A smaller version of the NYSE is the American Stock Exchange (AMEX), which also is located in Manhattan's financial district. Both are considered national exchanges, although the NYSE trades 15 to 20 times more shares daily than the AMEX. Stocks also are traded on several major regional exchanges.

The AMEX was formed more than 50 years ago by a group of individuals who traded unlisted shares at an outdoor location referred to as the Outdoor Curb Market. Typically, AMEX firms are smaller and younger than those listed on the NYSE. These companies are frequently considered emerging growth companies, not yet seasoned enough for the Big Board. (Big Board is another name for the NYSE.)

Generally, the stocks of the largest companies are traded on the NYSE, with smaller ones traded on the AMEX. The number of shares traded has dramatically increased through the years. Prior to the 1960s, the average daily trading volume was less than 3 million shares. Daily volume averaged about 15 million during the first half of the

1970s, exceeded 30 million by 1980, and exceeded 100 million shares during the 1980s. Record volume occurred on October 20, 1987, with 608,120,000 shares traded. So far during 1997, daily volumes have averaged around 450 to 550 million shares.

NASDAQ (NATIONAL ASSOCIATION OF SECURITIES DEALERS AUTOMATED QUOTATION)

The term *over-the-counter*, or OTC, originated when securities were traded over the counters in the storefront offices of various dealers. The term is now a totally inaccurate description of how this market works. The fact is, the OTC market does not have centralized trading floors where all orders are processed, as do the NYSE and AMEX. Instead, trading is conducted through a centralized computer-telephone network linking dealers across the country, which is known as NASDAQ (National Association of Securities Dealers Automated Quotation). As the name suggests, the NASDAQ provides a computerized information network through which brokers, bankers, and other investment professionals can obtain up-to-the-minute price quotations on securities traded over the counter. You can find the daily listing of prices for over-the-counter stocks in many newspapers; these listings are provided by NASDAQ.

NASDAQ celebrated its 25th birthday in February, 1996. And, although somewhat tired from its exhaustive growth spurts over the past few years, NASDAQ appears to be primed for the next 25 years.

At its inception in 1971, NASDAQ was a small network of 100 or so securities firms that traded over-the-counter stocks via desktop terminals. At the time, 2,827 companies were traded on the exchange; today, that number has climbed to more than 5,507 dealers and in excess of 6,290 companies—some of them are the largest household names, including Microsoft, Intel, MCI Communications, and Amgen.

Due to the rapidly growing volume, NASDAQ completed a much needed high-tech upgrade in 1995, boosting its projected capacity to one billion shares a day. From January 1, 1996 to September 30, 1996, the NASDAQ traded a daily average of 541,019,000 shares.

NASDAQ has experienced growing pains along the way, especially in the last few years as volume rapidly outstripped the electronic board's capability to keep pace. But officials are optimistic that an internal reorganization and new oversight regulations will keep the NASDAQ on track in the coming years.

Before NASDAQ was in operation, brokers had to check the prices of over-the-counter stocks by calling three or four different dealers. Now they simply push a few buttons and the latest prices appear on their computers. Thus, dealers or traders can negotiate directly with one another and with customers.

HISTORY OF PERFORMANCE

Probably the best study of comparative investment results was undertaken by Roger Ibbotson and Rex Sinquefield, who studied records going back to 1926. They calculated the compound annual returns (including reinvested dividends and interest) of large and small company stocks, corporate and government bonds, and Treasury bills. They matched all the returns against each other and, for added measure, against the inflation rate.

Figure 4-1 shows the results through 1994, a period that includes the two biggest stock market crashes in history, plus the Great Depression, a world war, a world conflict or two, a presidential assassination, an oil embargo, and more. Stocks won by a large margin, with small company stocks edging out those of large companies by a couple of percentage points. Even that difference looms large when compounded over the years: $1 growing at 10% a year for 20 years becomes about $6.73. At 12%, it becomes $9.60. During the 67-year period covered by the graph in Figure 4-1, $1 invested in the S&P 500, an unmanaged index, would have grown to just $810.54, whereas the same $1 riding along with small stocks would have grown to more than $2842.77.

Figure 4-1   Stocks, Bonds, Bills, and Inflation 1925–1994

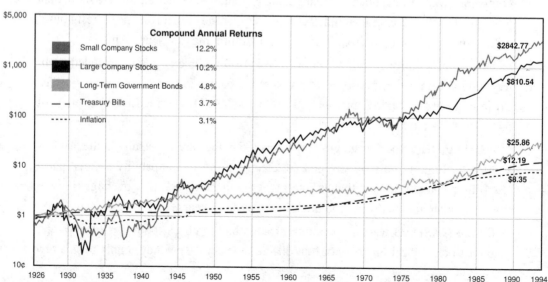

That's impressive, but unless your main concern is the financial welfare of your grandchildren, you probably prefer a somewhat faster pace. So here's the good news and something to think about: These results actually understate the long-term return you can reasonably expect to earn from blue chip stocks.

Why? Because the 10% return from large company stocks is based on the performance of all the companies in the S&P 500 with no attempt to separate the good companies from the bad. The same goes for the return from small company stocks, which means the dogs in this portfolio have lowered the return. This book will help you avoid those dogs!

What's more, the payoff from even mediocre stocks often beats the long-term averages, which of course covers bad times as well as good. From 1985 through 1989, the return on the 30 blue chip companies that make up the Dow topped 22% per year with dividends reinvested, and the 500 stocks in the S&P 500 followed closely behind. During the 1980s as a whole, Dow stocks returned 18% per year (the S&P 500 returned 17%), and in the 15-year period from 1975 through 1989, the blue chips of both the Dow and the S&P 500 returned an average of about 16%. The going has been a little tougher in the first half of the 1990s, with the S&P and the Dow returning earnings closer to their historical averages, with the exception of 1995 and 1996.

Dollars & $ense: One dollar invested in the S&P 500 at the end of 1925, unmanaged in any way, would be worth more than $1,370,000 at the end of 1996! And that's a compounded rate of return of only 10.7%!

In this book, I will show you how to pick stocks that can reasonably be expected to beat the averages during a decade in which it's widely believed that the stock market will not generate better-than-average returns. You don't have to beat the market by much to prosper. An ambitious but achievable goal is to do two to five percentage points better than the market. By that measure, your long-term goal should be to earn an average return of 12% to 15% or more—not every year, but on average. There is risk involved, as there is in all investments, but the important thing is to accept those risks as the only path to the higher returns you seek. And if you stick to the techniques described in this book, you can reduce those risks.

CASE STUDY

In 1993, a couple from St. Louis, in their 40s, were referred to me. Their kids were headed for college in two, four, and six years, and they were not happy with the results in their accounts. They asked me to manage their three children's college accounts (plus four more accounts). We began with approximately $85,000 in each account and began to purchase such stocks as Lilly, Hormel, Polaroid, Nike, and Lubrizol—all chosen based on good fundamentals. Working closely with the parents, we were able to fund the first year and half of their daughter's college, making distributions for books, living expenses, rent, and so on.

At the end of December 1996, the daughter's account was worth over $103,000, more than enough to fund the last two and a half years of her college. The second child, who begins college in September, 1997, now has an account value of $138,000— varied expenses, such as a new automobile, reduced the account. The third child, who begins college in two years, has an account worth $170,000.

Let's Remember This:

- ▶ To qualify as blue chip stocks, the company must have billions in assets, sales in more than one country, more than 250 million shares outstanding, have been in business for at least 15 years, and must be traded on a major exchange.

- ▶ The New York Stock Exchange (NYSE) is the largest, most well-known exchange; the American Stock Exchange (AMEX) is a smaller version of the NYSE. Over-the-counter (OTC) or NASDAQ (National Association of Securities Dealers Automated Quotations) usually lists the smaller, more aggressive-growth companies.

- ▶ Historically, stocks outperform all other asset classes, including bonds, real estate, and precious metals.

▼

UNDERSTANDING THE SYSTEM

WHAT WE ARE GOING TO TALK ABOUT IN THIS CHAPTER:

► What Kind of Blue Chip Stocks to Look For

► How to Pick Winning Blue Chip Stocks

► Using the Winning System

THE NUTS AND BOLTS: CREATING STOCK GUIDELINES

Investing in blue chip stocks, or any common stock for that matter, is appropriate for many, but not all, portfolios. For those investors who prefer fixed-income securities, namely those who are concerned about preservation of capital (the elderly, those incapable of making decisions, and/or those who can't stand the risk), it is imprudent to think that their portfolios should be loaded with stocks. For those who want to create a hedge against the ever-present risk of inflation, there are blue chip stocks that, over time, have outpaced inflation as well as afforded the investor capital appreciation. Of course, investing in stocks requires patience and an investment structure. Selecting the best companies for a portfolio requires the creation of a specific set of guidelines that can enhance a portfolio's performance. Additionally, by eliminating the companies that do not meet those guidelines, you can significantly reduce the risk.

Investing in the stock market can be very exciting or nerve-racking, depending on your point of view. Finding a company whose price soars to new highs by following the careful analysis and selection process outlined in this book creates a truly great feeling of satisfaction. This is not a pipe dream; it happens more often than not when everything falls properly into place.

What Stocks Should You Buy?

Here's something to think about: When you create your portfolio, what type of blue chip stocks should you look for? Will you, for example, lean toward a company whose products you recognize or whose services you've used? Take a step back for a moment and just consider the raw numbers. Are you going to look for companies that sell at their lows for the year, or for companies that sell at their highs? My advice is this: buy high and your stocks will go higher! It sounds crazy, but it's true. Allow me to explain.

Many investors like to purchase stocks at their lows (price-wise) using the logic that the price can't possibly go any lower, but can go higher if the company's fortunes turn around. In other words, buy low and hope to sell high. I prefer to look at that type of investing as bottom fishing for a sleeper, using emotional thinking. My experience, on the other hand, tells me to look at the cold, hard facts of why a particular company's stock hits bottom and is selling so cheaply, compared to where its price has been previously. There is always a reason why a stock is selling at the bottom of its range. There's no telling when or if this company will ever get its corporate act together sufficiently for its stock to appreciate in value. I can tell you that most investors love to bottom fish because of the thrill of seeing a low-cost stock rise. Much of this kind of investing is based not on facts, but on hopes and prayers.

Stick With the Winners

You can look at it another way. There is a reason why a given company's stock is making new highs day after day, week after week, for months. The driving force is usually good earnings and/or good corporate news that sends stock prices higher. In other words, higher revenues and higher earnings equate to higher stock prices. The great companies of the world don't sell at $20 one day and $100 the next. It's a progression of increasing revenues and earnings and/or good news that moves prices from $50 to $51, then to $52 to $53, and higher.

I realize that this type of investing defies the conventional wisdom, but here's my own guidance: The most important thing to understand when investing is that the underlying objective is to make money. And you can make money by playing the game by the rules that favor you, not by rules that favor the house.

Here's why. Say you are given unlimited resources to organize a professional ball club. What would you do? First, you would hire the best management team money could buy. Next, you would obtain the best players, who would increase your odds of winning. And to keep the odds of winning in your favor, you would hire the exceptional players: the Michael Jordans, the Babe Ruths, the Hank Aarons, the Joe Montanas. They can win the games for you. And winning is the objective, whether it be in the business world or in your private life.

Well, it's the same story in the stock market. Acquire the best companies you can to make yourself a winner in this game as well. How do you do that? By creating an investment structure utilizing effective guidelines and parameters, in much the same way you would build a winning ball team. In this manner, you can increase those all-important odds in your favor. When looking for a company for me and my clients to invest in, I look for a company that is one of the best—if not the best—in that industry and a company whose earnings growth rate appears to be accelerating. Then I further analyze the company's past as to revenues and earnings, and especially as to how management is coping with day-to-day operations. I scrutinize past history very closely to determine if it fits my guidelines and parameters as a company worthy to be included in my basket of stock holdings. If the company's past history has been excellent, and if its standing in its industry is sustaining the potential for continued stock price increases through astute management and demand for the company's products, then it should continue in its leadership.

THE SYSTEM

So where do you go from here? Now you get to the real nuts and bolts of analyzing and picking good quality blue chip stocks. Each company to be analyzed is chosen on the basis of its past history. Some say that past performance is no guarantee of future performance. But for an investor, if a company has been successful in increasing its earnings annually, it stands to reason that earnings growth could continue—provided the company continues to do the same things that made it successful in the past.

Before analyzing a company that would qualify for purchase into your portfolio, use the following guidelines to help you pick blue chip stocks that can increase the odds of making lots of money in the stock, and simultaneously reducing your chances of buying duds.

- ▶ *Annual increase in earnings per share.* This is the company's bottom line, the profits earned after taxes and payment of dividends and interest to all stock-holders and bondholders. Dividing net profits by the number of common shares outstanding during the period being measured gives you *earnings per share* (EPS), a key number for evaluating any company. Earnings are also the company's chief resource for paying dividends to shareholders and for reinvesting in business growth. I search for companies whose EPS increase year after year after year. Consistent EPS in both good times and bad, that is, in different business cycles, reflects good management and tells me that the company can sustain its growth rate, theoretically reducing the risk of owning that particular stock.

- ▶ *Annual increase in revenues.* Just as increases in EPS can ensure the success of a particular company, so too do annual increases in revenues. Consecutive annual increases in revenues reveal the continuing demand for the company's products or services and that management continues to be aggressive in its game plan.

- ▶ *Minimal long-term debt.* The debt-equity ratio shows how much leverage, or debt, a company is carrying compared with shareholders' equity. For example, if a company has $1 billion in shareholders' equity and $100 million in debt, its debt-equity ratio is 10%. In general, the lower this figure the better, although the definition of an acceptable debt load varies from industry to industry. The best scenario is for a company to possess no long-term debt. Blue chip stocks, due to their size, usually possess long-term debt, but the important point to make is that if there is debt, it should not be excessive. Excessive debt will inhibit the growth in EPS. Increases in a company's debt can impede its growth and/or acquisition potentials.

- ▶ *A current ratio of 1:1 or greater.* A company should have sufficient current assets (cash and/or cash equivalents that can be converted to cash very quickly) to pay off all current liabilities (short-term obligations, such as monthly bills, mortgage payments, and so on), and have assets left over for other corporate needs. The greater the ratio, the greater the reserves there are to cope with day-to-day realities of business.

▶ *Annual increase in dividends.* If a company can grow revenues and EPS, it stands to reason that it can increase dividends paid to shareholders. Dividends are *lagniappe* (a little extra on the side); companies reward shareholders for having faith in management and their company.

▶ *Annual increase in book values.* Also called *shareholder's equity,* book value is nothing more than the difference between the company's assets and its liabilities. Book value per share is the company's assets less liabilities divided by the number of shares of common stock outstanding. Normally, the price of a company's stock is higher than its book value, and stocks may be recommended as cheap because they are selling at or below book value. Such stocks have often attracted takeover bids from big investors and corporate raiders, which in turn attracted other investors who bid up the price of the shares. A company also may be selling below book value because the company shows little promise. The optimum indicator that the value of a company is increasing is the growth in its book value. It is optimum when the book value shows annual increases, which supports the premise that the company is growing and that management continues to do a good job.

▶ *Higher highs of stock prices annually.* When EPS, revenues, and book values increase consecutively, it should reflect in higher highs in the market price of the stock.

▶ *Higher lows of stock prices annually.* Similarly, if higher highs reflect steadily growing EPS, revenues, and book values, then higher lows should follow. These are excellent signals of earnings growth.

An Example

In this section, you learn how to analyze a blue chip company with present and future potential. Carefully considering the fundamentals of a company is important in determining whether a stock fits into a portfolio based on preset guidelines for selecting blue chip stocks. For this example, you will dissect each component of a blue chip stock called the Soft Drink Company (SDC).

You first need to learn what its business is and what its potential is for future growth. SDC is a leading soft drink company, it produces fruit juices, and it's part owner of a bottling company. SDC recently completed a major restructuring process. Its bottling partners are in virtually every corner of the Earth and possess the financial and managerial resources to achieve the goals set. As situations change, so too does SDC's structural improvements. Global growth is its goal and it is solidly located in eight major distribution areas around the world to take advantage of its customers demand for SDC's brands.

SDC's potential in various markets is boundless. For example, the per capita consumption in China is four 8 ounce servings per person annually and the population is more than 1.2 billion; India's per capita consumption is two 8 ounce servings per person per year with more than 900 million in the population; Indonesia's per capita is one 8 ounce serving with a population of 200 million; and Russia's per capita is one 6 ounce serving with a population of 147 million. Include potential increases in domestic consumption into the equation and this spells huge potential for years to come. It is not hard to see why this company deserves a closer look.

The financial data, or fundamentals, are the most important things to observe; good fundamentals drive stock prices. The fundamentals, when analyzing stocks over the long term (in excess of three or more years), are the telling factors to determine whether a company is worth holding onto for the long term. Management has the responsibility of finding new business and keeping business profitable so revenues and earnings will continue to grow at a reasonable rate to satisfy shareholders and to keep dividends increasing as well. The trick is to find those types of companies and hold on to them for as long as they perform the task of growing. This could be for years and years, despite economic downturns. Good quality companies can grow in all types of economic climates. What may be effected is its stock price with corrections occurring in the stock market, but if the companies fundamentals remain in tact, it may be prudent to hold onto your holdings. Higher consecutive quarterly EPS will ensure higher prices in the stocks you hold following potential corrections in the market. If the stock price falls during a correction in the market, it just may be the opportunity to add to your position.

Table 5.1 is a profile of SDC. It details each category you should initially consider in determining whether to buy stock in a company. These factors will tell you immediately whether you should go any further with your analysis. (This information is readily available on most publicly traded companies; see Chapter 9 for more details.)

Table 5-1   The Fundamentals of the Soft Drink Company*

Dec	EPS	REV(B)	NET(B)	BV/SH	DIV
1996*	$.71	$9.48	$1.76	N/A	$.25
1995	1.18	18.02	2.99	$1.77	.44
1994	.99	16.17	2.56	1.74	.39
1993	.84	13.96	2.19	1.55	.34
1992	.71	13.74	1.88	1.24	.28

*For the six months ending June 30, 1996

Dec tells me that this company's fiscal year ends every year on the last day of December. Most companies' fiscal years end on December 31, the same as the calendar year, while others close their books during a time of the year when business has slowed due to seasonal conditions. For example, a retailer would not want to close out the year at the end of November, between Thanksgiving and Christmas; instead it would close the books during a lull period, such as January 31.

EPS is the net profits of the company divided into the amount of shares outstanding. EPS is critical because it tells you if the company is growing in profitability. As you can see, from 1992 through 1995, EPS increased annually from $.71 to $.84 to $.99 to $1.18, an annual compound growth rate of more than 18% during that four-year period. For the first six months of 1996, EPS was $.71 and on track to set a record for the full year. Exceptional!

Rev, or *revenues,* is the sales of the company in billions of dollars (the *B* following Rev and Net stands for billions). In this case, Rev increased from $13.74 billion in 1992 to $13.96 billion in 1993, to $16.17 billion in 1994, and to $18.02 billion in 1995. This represents an annual compound growth rate in excess of 9%. If EPS grows faster than revenues, it tells you that the company is managing growth well and margins are getting better through efficiencies. It appears you are going to see more revenues for the full year of 1996 than 1995 because their six month figures are ahead of 1995.

Net is the *net income,* or profit, in billions of dollars. When you divide the net income into the number of shares outstanding, you get the EPS. Net income for SDC increased from $1.88 billion to $2.19 billion to $2.56 billion to $2.99 billion from 1992 through 1995. For the first six months of 1996, net income also was way ahead of the first six months of 1995.

Note: Although I have assigned fictitious names to all the companies used as examples, all are real companies and the figures given are actual figures.

BV/SH, or *book value per share*, is the common shareholder's value of the company on a per-share basis. It's calculated by subtracting liabilities from assets and dividing the remainder by the company's outstanding shares of stock. For SDC, the BV/SH increased from $1.24 in 1992 to $1.55 in 1993, to $1.74 in 1994, and to $1.77 in 1995. SDC has been really impressive over the past four years, and it appears poised to continue.

DIV, or *dividend*, is the amount of corporate earnings paid annually to shareholders, in this case $.28 per share in 1992, $.34 in 1993, $.39 in 1994, and $.44 in 1995. In 1996, dividends increased to a higher level than in 1995.

Now look at the increases in SDC's stock price during the same four-year period (see Table 5-2). As mentioned, *stock prices are driven by earnings,* and these figures bear this out. The growth rate in earnings and revenues resulted in its stock price highs escalating from $22.68 in 1992 to $40.18 in 1995. The stock price lows during the same period rose from $17.78 in 1992 to $24.37 in 1995. Imagine if you bought SDC at its mid-range in 1992 of $20.23 and sold it at the mid-range in 1995 for $32.27—you would have realized a 59% return on your money. Pretty good, and only because of the driving force of the earnings. And how about the share earnings for SDC?

Table 5-2   The Soft Drink Company Stock Prices for 5-year Period

Year	High	Low
1996	$53.12	$36.06
1995	40.18	24.37
1994	26.75	19.43
1993	22.56	18.75
1992	22.68	17.78

Table 5-3 continues the analysis.

Table 5-3   Soft Drink Company Current Share Earnings

6 months June 1995	$.71 / $.61
July 1, 1995 through June 30, 1996	$1.28
P/E	36
5-Year Growth Percentage	+17%

6 Months June 1995 means that in the six months ending in June 1995, the EPS was $.71 versus $.61 in the same six-month period in 1994. This is a healthy 16.4% growth rate.

July 1, 1995 through June 30, 1996, indicates the EPS of $1.28 during the indicated 12-month period. The company appears to be on track in its upward growth spiral.

P/E, the *price/earnings multiple* (also called a *price/earnings ratio*), is calculated by dividing the EPS over the last 12 months ($1.28) into the present price of the stock ($47.00). The P/E is simply a measure of the relationship between the price of the stock and its EPS. A high ratio of 40, 50, or more, usually means the stock may be too high in relation to earnings, or that the earnings growth rate may be accelerating. If the P/E is in fact too high, you may see some decrease in the company's stock price if the rest of the companies in the same industry are selling at a lower P/E. My preference is not to buy exceptionally high P/E stocks. If the P/E of the blue chip is less than 30 times the company's annual growth rate in earnings, I may consider it as a possible purchase candidate. A low P/E of 8, 10, or 12 could indicate little or no growth potential, or might simply indicate an industry which, as a group, sells at low P/Es.

Money Talks: Utility stocks tend to act more like bonds in the marketplace, although they often are very large companies. Utilities have high debt payments due to their large borrowing habits and consequently are highly susceptible to interest rate swings.

Low P/Es usually include companies whose earnings are stagnant, such as utility companies (whose debt structures remain high in relation to revenues). For example, some utility companies have long-term debt higher than their revenues, which is unacceptable in my scheme. My preference is for blue chip companies to have their long-term debt be less than 20% of their revenues.

Dollars & Sense: If you want to own utility stocks, consider them as bonds rather than blue chip or other stocks in your portfolio allocation.

Sometimes a company will decide to reward their shareholders by paying out a certain amount of money in the form of *dividends* (see Table 5-4). Suppose a company has made more earnings than they anticipated and has money left over. SDC retained these earnings for internal growth and its board of directors decided to pay a per-share dividend to shareholders of $.28 per share in 1992. As you can see, the company increased its dividend annually from $.28 in 1992 all the way up to $.50 in 1996. SDC increased its dividend annually as earnings increased. When companies have bad years, they either keep the dividend intact or reduce it to retain as much money as they can for operating the company (this is called *retained earnings*).

Table 5-4 Soft Drink Company Dividends

Year	*Dividend*
1996	$.50
1995	.44
1994	.39
1993	.34
1992	.28

Dollars & $ense: Most blue chip stocks have a reinvestment option. Reinvest the dividend to increase your wealth and to take advantage of dollar cost averaging.

Money Talks: *Dollar cost averaging* is a system of making periodic purchases of an investment. By buying at all price levels, your cost will be averaged.

In Table 5-5, *1996 Rng* tells you that the high and low price range of the stock so far in 1996 is a $52.50 high and a $36.06 low. This enables you to make comparisons with the prior year's figures, to see if the price of the stock is higher or lower than in previous years. It's just a guide for you as to what the stock price was during the preceding year.

Table 5-5 Market Action of the Soft Drink Company's Stock

1996 Rng (through 9/1/96)	$52.50 High	$36.06 Low
Avg. Daily Vol.	2,385,584	
Beta	.8	
Inst. Holdings	48%	

Avg. Daily Vol., or *average daily volume,* tells you how many shares are traded daily. SDC trades 2,385,584 shares on an average day. If volume picks up appreciably, it could be either good or bad, depending on where the stock price is going when the volume is heavier. If the stock appreciates more than double or triple normal volume, it means the stock is in the accumulation mode and could very well move higher. Conversely, if it goes lower on heavy volume, it signifies that people are selling and the shares are under pressure to go lower.

Beta is a mathematical measure of the sensitivity of rates of return on a given stock, as compared with rates of return on the market as a whole. This is a measure of stock market risk. A beta of 1 equals the market. A high beta (more than 1) indicates moderate or high price volatility as compared to the market as a whole; a beta less than 1 forecasts the possibility of less than 1% change in the return on an asset for every 1% change in the return of the market. SDC has a beta of .8, which means that for every 1% the stock market moves either up of down, SDC's stock will move .8% respectively. That means there is less volatility in this company than in the market as a whole. Again, good news about the company tends to move the stock higher and bad news tends to move it lower.

Inst Holdings, or *institutional holdings,* is the amount of stock held by institutions as opposed to individuals. Institutions hold 48% of SDC's stock. These institutions include pension plans, profit sharing plans, or mutual funds. Institutional representation, whether it's 25% or 50% or 75%, is something you want to be aware of. As long as the earnings are improving quarterly as well as annually, then institutions will usually hold their positions. If an institution sells its position, it obviously could adversely move the stock downward.

There are many indicators that warrant close watch of a company's stock, to ensure as much as you can that your money makes money for you—as much money as possible.

Table 5-6 shows a part of the balance sheet. *Cur Ratio*, or *current ratio,* is the relationship between current assets and current liabilities, which is calculated by dividing current liabilities into current assets. Current assets and current liabilities include marketable securities, accounts receivable, accounts payable, inventories, prepaid expenses, and other items that will be converted into cash within one year. The higher the current ratio, the higher a company's liquidity (and safety).

Table 5-6 The Soft Drink Company's Balance Sheet	
Cur Ratio	.81
Lt Dt (B)	1,149,000,000
Shrs (B)	2,493,000,000
Financial report as of	6/30/96

SDC's current ratio is .81, which means it has less current assets than current liabilities. Although this is not a favorable sign, consider the fact that their business is a cash cow, with $18 billion in revenues and increasing, not to mention increasing EPS and book value, as well. It is my feeling that current assets will grow as short-term liabilities are reduced worldwide and margins widen due to reduced expenses.

Lt Dt (B) indicates the company's long-term debt in billions of dollars. According to my investment guidelines, the best situation is a company that has limited debt to worry about, because debt simply adds to the potential problems of a company's growth. As you can see, long-term debt in this case amounts to $1.1 billion.

Shrs (B) tells you how many shares, in billions, the company has sold to the public and to institutions. For a company whose revenues are more than $18 billion, 2.493 billion shares outstanding is sizable but not excessive. To make it more palatable to those who want to own stock in this company, SDC recently split its stock 2 for 1. Splitting a stock simply doubles the number of shares (if it's a 2-for-1 split) and reduces the market value of the share by half. (On the surface, a stock split does not change a shareholder's financial stake in the company. The shareholder's ownership percentage of outstanding shares remains the same, only now each share is worth less. For example, if I give you two $10 bills in exchange for your $20, your cash value remains at $20, even though you have doubled the pieces of paper representing your $20 in value. A 2-for-1 stock split works the same way. While the stock split itself may not deliver any financial gain to the shareholder, accompanying events can produce situations that create additional value that can translate into significant investment gains. First, as stock prices rise to lofty levels, they tend to get beyond the range of many individual investors who like to purchase in increments of 100 shares. A stock split is designed to reduce the company's stock price and once again place it within a reasonable price range for the small investor. This action can create additional demand for the company's stock, and demand drives stock prices in some instances.

NYSE statistics seem to support the theory that individual investors prefer to acquire stocks in reasonable price ranges. Management also likes stock splits because the increase in the number of shares after a split broadens the company's shareholder base, making the firm less susceptible to price swings caused by traders and institutional investors. A broad shareholder base also can be a deterrent to unwanted takeover bids.

Stock splits are popular with growth companies that want to convert capital to expand their business instead of paying out dividends. The assumption is that cash used to fund operations, research, development, and strategic acquisitions will enhance shareholder value more than cash dividends.

The stock split also is a signal of good news. After all, the stock split would not have occurred if the company's stock price had not risen dramatically based on good earnings performance or at least the prospects of better times ahead. The approval of a stock split also represents a vote of confidence by the board of directors that management can maintain its record of improving operating and financial results. The anticipation of increased earnings and dividends, as discussed earlier, can add a lot of fuel to the company's stock price. According to an NYSE study, stocks that have split appreciate two and a half times faster than stocks that have not split, for up to seven years after the split.

Dollars & Sense: Remember, stock can split to increase the outstanding number of shares, or it can split to reduce the outstanding number of shares. This is called a *reverse split.*

For individual investors, the major point to remember is that the board of directors vote for stock splits because they believe in the continuation of the company's operating results and in improving earnings and dividends. It's your job to determine when this optimism is warranted.

Tracking companies after the announcement to split their stock is one way to capitalize on the opportunity. If you can ferret out upcoming stock split candidates and invest in them before the announcement date, you can gain an additional edge and put yourself in the position to earn more impressive returns, assuming you pick the right candidates.

In this regard, you should research companies that have a record of successful operations and a past history of stock splits and accompanying cash dividend increases.

If you're investing in the company for the long haul, make sure it has strong enough fundamentals to keep revenues, earnings, and dividend growth on track after the split.

The analysis of all the terms you have just looked at tells you most of what you need to know to make a decision as to whether to include SDC stock in your portfolio. Clearly, SDC has created some excellent profits for my clients and is one of my big winners. SDC possesses all the advantages that a superstar contributes to making your ball club a winner. My future clients will own SDC as well.

CASE STUDY

After attending a seminar for women that I held in 1993, a 68-year old woman opened an account of $75,000 with me. She wanted a combination of growth and income, and she determined how much income she needed monthly from her investments. After this criteria was met, we invested the remaining funds in her account in blue chip stocks. Again, due to sound stock selecting, monitoring, and market action, her account has grown to $184,000, using such investments as Gillette, Coca Cola, the Bank of New York, and Pepsi. We have become good friends, and she often tells me how grateful she is to me for giving her a better quality of life due to our investment decisions. Certainly her retirement has been enhanced by the good fortune of having stocks, a sound portfolio, and a methodology to make consistent investment decisions.

Let's Remember This:

► Buy high and watch your blue chips go higher.

► Stick with winners—let your profits run.

► Look for the following:

1. annual increase in EPS
2. annual increase in revenues
3. minimal long-term debt
4. current ratio of 1:1 or better
5. annual increase in dividends
6. annual increase in book values
7. higher highs of stock prices annually
8. higher lows of stock prices annually

▼

INVESTMENT STRUCTURE

WHAT WE ARE GOING TO TALK ABOUT IN THIS CHAPTER:

- ▶ Review the Winning System Guidelines

- ▶ The Best Way to Analyze Two Different Companies Using the Winning System

- ▶ How to Make a Buying Recommendation On the Two Analyzed Companies

STRUCTURE FOR INVESTING

As I have mentioned, blue chip stocks are appropriate for many, but not all, portfolios. There also are those investors who are very aggressive, trying to make a quick buck in commodities or in stock selling for less than one dollar, as well as those who have the propensity to invest without a set plan, rather like collecting sea shells at the beach: You pick up whatever catches your eye regardless of whether it complements your collection or not.

Like most good investments, blue chip stocks require patience, particularly because of their slower growth rate than, say, small capitalization stocks. Blue chip stocks' rate of growth simply trods along due to their age and size. The fact remains that most blue chip stocks are characterized by some degree of uncertainty as to future growth potential. But if you know how to select and value blue chip stocks, they can provide excellent protection against the ever-increasing cost of living. In other words, they can give you your hedge against inflation.

Before you look at four-year histories of two different companies and analyze them, I want to again stress the guidelines and parameters I use.

Take another look at the following list of qualifications that a stock must have to increase the odds of succeeding in the stock market (for more information, refer to Chapter 5):

▶ Annual increase in earnings per share (EPS)

▶ Annual increase in revenues

▶ Minimal long-term debt

▶ Current ratio of 1:1 (or better)

▶ Annual increase in dividends

▶ Annual increase in book values

▶ Higher highs of stock prices annually

▶ Higher lows of stock prices annually

A careful consideration of financial data and market action (discussed below) is important in making a determination as to whether a stock fits into our portfolio based on our investment structure. Let's dissect each component of the blue chip stock, the Soft Drink Company (SDC). Utilizing each of the elements discussed to this point, you will see a complete picture of this blue chip gem.

The following is a profile of SDC. Table 6-1 details each category I initially consider in determining whether to buy stock in a company. These factors immediately tell me whether I should go any further with my analysis. All of the terms and definitions used in the following text were discussed in Chapter 5; these definitions are being used here only as comparisons for the example of a blue chip stock that does *not* meet the guidelines.

Table 6-1 The Soft Drink Company					
Dec	EPS	REV(B)	NET(B)	BV/SH	DIV
1996*	$.71	$9.48	$1.76	N/A	$.25
1995	1.18	18.02	2.99	$1.77	.44
1994	.99	16.17	2.56	1.74	.39
1993	.84	13.96	2.19	1.55	.34
1992	.71	13.74	1.88	1.24	.28

*For the six months ending June 30, 1996

Dec tells me that this company's fiscal year ends every year on the last day of December.

EPS is the net profits of the company divided into the amount of shares outstanding. As you can see, from 1992 to 1995 EPS increased annually from $.71 to $.84 to $.99 to $1.18, and finally to $.71 for the first six months of 1996 (versus $.61 during the same six-month period of 1995).

Revenues have grown as well, from $13.74 billion in 1992 to $18.02 billion in 1995; they're on track to a new record in 1996 with the first six months at $9.48 billion.

Net income rose annually from $1.88 billion in 1992 to $2.19 billion in 1993, to $2.56 billion in 1994, to $2.99 billion in 1995, and to $1.76 billion for the first six months of 1996.

Dividends have risen annually from $.28 to $.34 to $.39 to $.44 for the same years from 1992 through 1995. So far in 1996, SDC has paid $.25 per share or $.50 for the full year.

Book values also have grown from $1.24 in 1992 to $1.77 in 1995.

The company continues to prosper under excellent management and increased sales from all of their product lines. Based on their growth rate alone, a stock like this could remain in an investor's portfolio indefinitely, provided such a pattern continues.

The market action shows the price range of SDC from a high and low in 1992 of $22.68 and $17.78, respectively. Increases in higher highs and higher lows occurred also, from 1993 through 1995 and so far into 1996.

The market action depicted in Table 6-2 shows that the 1996 range in the stock price has been from a high of $53.12 to a low of $36.06—a continuation of SDC's price increase over the past few years at least. Their average volume stands at 2,385,584 shares per day.

Table 6-2	The Soft Drink Company Stock Prices for 5-year Period	
Year	*High*	*Low*
1996	$53.12	$36.06
1995	40.18	24.37
1994	26.75	19.43
1993	22.56	18.75
1992	22.68	17.78

The beta stands at 0.8, which means that for every 1% the overall market moves, this blue chip will move 0.8%, which is not as volatile as the overall market. Institutional holdings are at 48% of the total outstanding shares, which means that 1,145,080 shares are held by those institutions.

Market Action

In Table 6-3, the current ratio is .81. As I stressed earlier, SDC is a cash cow and their cash flow is enough to handle any sort of expense incurred by the company. They are reducing their long-term debt by cutting expenses and are in the process of buying back some of their outstanding shares. Their long-term debt stands at $1,149,000,000, which is not overbearing for an $18 billion company.

Table 6-3 Market Action of the Soft Drink Company

Rng (through 9/1/96)	$52.50	$36.06
Cur Ratio		.81
Avg. Vol.		2,385,584
Beta		.8
Inst, Holdings		48%

Dollars & Sense: When a corporation buys back its own stock, it effectively reduces the shares outstanding, which enhances the value of the shares remaining in investors' portfolios.

This is a report of the company's financial condition as of June 30, 1996. If you are a conservative investor who wants growth and odds that favor you, then look for stocks similar to this blue chip that possess fundamentals that mirror this company. At this point, SDC fits all my parameters assigned to blue chip stock and, in fact, has been an excellent addition to portfolios I have managed for years. The growth and dividends have continued and the stock has appreciated in value. What more could you ask for?

For comparison, take a look at another blue chip stock, called The Retail Corporation (TRC). TRC is a corporation that is a major retailer of general merchandise, including shoe and apparel chains comprised of more than 8,000 outlets. TRC has been a household name for years; most everyone has shopped there. Unfortunately, TRC has not been able to keep up with its competition.

Take a look at its four-year history so you can make your own determination of whether to invest in TRC (see Table 6-4).

Dec	EPS	REV(B)	NET(B)	DIV	BV/SH
		Table 6-4 The Retail Corporation			
1996*	Nil	$3.676	Nil	$0	N/A
1995	$–1.23	8.224	$–164	.15	$8.53
1994	.36	8.293	47	.88	9.18
1993	–3.76	9.626	–495	1.15	9.34
1992	2.14	9.962	280	1.11	14.68

*For the six months ending June 30, 1996

As you can see, TRC's EPS has been all over the place, earning $2.14 in 1992, losing $3.76 in 1993, earning $.36 in 1994, and again losing $1.23 in 1995. For the six months ending June 30, 1996, EPS was nil. It appears that the roller coaster ride continues!

These revenues reflect a decrease in business, which means that either TRC has closed unprofitable stores to reduce losses or the competition is winning customers away. Revenues went from $9.962 billion in 1992 to $9.626 billion in 1993 to $8.293 billion in 1994 and to $8.224 billion in 1995. Revenues are down from $3.716 billion in the first six months of 1995 to $3.676 billion in the same period of 1996.

So EPS are all over the spectrum and revenues are on the decline. Net income, as you would expect, has not been impressive either, with $280 million in 1992, a deficit of $495 million in 1993, $47 million in 1994, and another deficit of $164 million in 1995. During the first six months of 1996, net income was non-existent compared to the deficit in 1995 of $91 million for the same six-month period.

Additionally, dividends have dropped during the same period between 1992 through 1995 to $1.11, $1.15, $0.88, and $0.15, respectively. So far in 1996, there have been no dividends declared. Finally, you can see that TRC's book value per share decreased annually from $14.68 in 1992, to $9.34 in 1993, to $9.18 in 1994, and to $8.53 in 1995.

What you see here is a blue chip company going in the wrong direction. If TRC continues to lose market share and can't turn around, then I suspect that stock prices will continue to deteriorate. Speaking of market price, take a look at what has happened to TRC's share price over the past four and a half years (see Table 6-5).

Table 6-5   The Retail Corporation Stock Prices for 5-year Period

Year	High	Low
1996	$25.25	$9.37
1995	19.37	12.25
1994	26.25	12.87
1993	32.75	20.50
1992	22.68	17.78

Just as you suspected? In Table 6-5, stock prices were driven by earnings, although in this case the direction was downward. The highs increased from $22.68 in 1992 to $32.75 in 1993 to $26.25 in 1994 to $19.37 in 1995. In 1996, the high was $25.25. The lows were even more dramatic, dropping from $17.78 in 1992 all the way to $9.37 in 1996!

The lesson here: Pay attention to companies who continue to show annual increases in EPS, revenues, dividends, and book values. Stay away from companies that do not fit your guidelines for picking winners in the stock market and you will increase those all-important odds that favor earning profits.

Now that you have analyzed two blue chip stocks (one that fits the model of my guidelines and one that does not), here is one last side-by-side comparison that reveals an even more startling picture (see Table 6-6).

Table 6-6   The Fundamentals of Both the Soft Drink Company and The Retail Corporation

	The Soft Drink Company				The Retail Corporation			
	1992	1993	1994	1995	1992	1993	1994	1995
EPS	$.71	$.84	$.99	$1.18	$2.14	$-.376	$.36	$-1.23
Revenues (B)	13.74	13.96	16.17	18.02	9.96	9.63	8.29	8.22
Net Income (B)	1.88	2.19	2.56	2.99	280	-.495	47	-164
BV/SH	1.24	1.55	1.74	1.77	14.68	9.34	9.18	8.53
Dividends	.28	.34	.39	.44	1.11	1.15	.88	.15

As you can see in Table 6-6, SDC has increases annually for four consecutive years in all categories from EPS, revenues, net income, book values, and dividends. These increases drove stock price increases every year. Conversely, TRC performed poorly from a corporate standpoint with deteriorating fundamentals that have led to an annual decrease in its stock prices. Which company would you have wanted in your portfolio over the past four years?

Investor beware: Appreciation in stock prices in previous years (due to increased revenue and earnings) does not guarantee future growth and stock price increases. On the other hand, if you use my investment structure, I believe your odds will be greatly increased. You will see corrections (market drops) along the way, but it certainly appears that this bull market still has a long way to go—perhaps through the turn of the century and beyond. With corporate earnings increasing (due in no small part to restructuring within the past few years) and with interest rates remaining the same or trending lower due to a modest inflation rate, the ingredients are in place to be able to benefit in the stock market. The three examples shown (modest inflation, interest rates mirroring inflation, and higher corporate earnings) stand out as the most important reasons to trigger higher stock prices.

In addition, we are living in a unique time in history. With 70 million baby boomers reaching retirement age within the next 10 years, there is a huge amount of money pouring into the stock market. The stock market seems to be the only viable investment where you can invest your money without tying it up for long periods of time. Your liquidity is in terms of days, as compared to real estate, for example, where there is no telling how liquid a property may be. Imagine that those 70 million baby boomers invest $5,000 annually—that equates to $350 billion a year or more than $29 billion of new money invested in the stock market monthly! This is another very big reason, in my opinion, that the market is rising on balance and the corrections are not as drastic as some people had thought.

Remember that prices of blue chip stocks are driven by earnings and that the best time to invest is when the overall market is going up. Today, with the economy growing only slightly, due in part to the approaching $6 trillion budget deficit, we can probably expect a continued increase of stock prices.

On top of all this, supply far outweighs demand. With the endless supply of goods, it appears that inflation just might remain low through the end of this decade and beyond. It's a good bet that this scenario spells the continuation of the bull market. Corporate earnings increases across most sectors of the market could surprise a lot of investors as to the overall strength in the stock market.

Remember, increases in a company's growth must not only support the stock price, but also increase its stock price over time. And consider this, in 1995, the U.S. stock market posted its largest increase in recent memory, gaining some 35%—and it's still going strong. On the other hand, the economy has only grown at a 1.4% rate and consumer consumption is lackluster. This is because a healthy stock market usually reflects the *wealth effect*, a theory that rising stock market prices make people feel wealthier and thus spend more. So, what is going on? A recent study by economist James M. Poterba of the Massachusetts Institute of Technology and Andrew A. Samwick of Dartmouth College may hold the answer. The study, based on Federal Reserve data, shows that stock ownership is highly concentrated. In other words, as shown in Figure 6-1, a mere 10% of all households own an estimated 90% of all shares. And looking at the opposite side of the coin, 80% of all households own a mere 2% of all shares. Because the greater percentage of stock ownership resides in the portfolios of the wealthy, there is no corresponding increase in consumer spending (the rich, it seems, aren't buying more Rolls Royces). This could explain the lackluster growth of the economy and the growing sense of economic anxiety felt by many Americans.

Figure 6-1   Equity Investment by Household

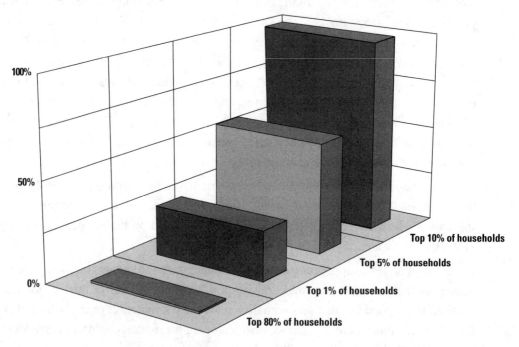

So, in spite of the so-called market boom, many Americans still need to beef up their savings and investment portfolios. Otherwise the distance between the haves and the have-nots will continue to widen.

CASE STUDY

Upon the passing of one of my clients in 1991, her daughter came to me not knowing what to do with her $100,000 inheritance. Following hours of education, she decided to point toward growth because she was recently married and was pregnant with her first child. She and her husband moved to Georgia, where her husband works as a CPA. Today, six years later, her account is worth more than $345,000 and she has begun to annually gift the shares to her two daughters. Because she has never had the kind of wealth she currently enjoys in her investment account, she continues to be delighted by the investment results. My future clients should be so fortunate.

LET'S REMEMBER THIS:

▶ Careful consideration of financial data is critical. Stock prices are driven by earnings.

▶ Baby boomers are investing in stocks and demand is greater than supply.

▶ Corporate earnings are rising and inflation should remain low.

C H A P T E R 7

▼

RESOURCES

WHAT WE ARE GOING TO TALK ABOUT IN THIS CHAPTER:

- ▶ What Information is Available to Investors

- ▶ Where to Find This Information

- ▶ How to Evaluate the Quality of the Information You Receive

RESOURCES

To pick the best blue chip stocks for your portfolio, you will need information. Where do you get it? And what does it look like? There are many sources of information and misinformation about investing. One highly publicized source is whoever is "hot" on Wall Street.

ADVICE FROM THE PROS

On January 6, 1981, stock market guru Joseph Granville told subscribers to his newsletter to sell everything. The next day, the Dow dropped 23 points—a substantial sell-off at that time. The following day it fell another 15 points. This call established Granville as the most prominent forecaster on Wall Street. However, his reputation quickly faded the next year when he missed the great bull market starting in 1982.

Money Talks: To illustrate just how pervasive his appeal was, Joseph Granville dressed as Moses and was carrying two stone tablets when he appeared on the Tonight Show with Johnny Carson!

In the late 1980s, Robert Prechter and the Elliott Wave Theory became vogue. On July 7, 1986, Prechter told his subscribers to sell everything right away. That day the Dow plummeted almost 62 points, the record at that time for a one-day drop. He quickly turned bullish, predicting the Dow would rise to 3,600. His following rapidly diminished after the crash of October 1987.

Newsletters Foretell Fortunes

Another very popular source of information for investors is the newsletter. Millions of investors subscribe to hundreds of newsletters annually, paying anywhere from $50 to $1,000 a year for advice that varies widely in quality and usefulness.

Many investment newsletters make extravagant claims about their performance and suggest that following their advice will lead to stock market riches. You should be leery of such claims. On the other hand, some newsletters can be useful—if you use them for the right reasons and in the right ways.

The various mailings reflect nearly every approach to investing. Many use technical analysis, which attempts to predict future prices based on the patterns of past prices, to make their recommendations. Others use fundamental analysis, analyzing earnings, cash flow, asset value, and other basic financial data to make their recommendations.

Still others are more specialized, focusing on small stocks, stock options, charts, insider trading, mutual funds, or other particular areas of investments. Newsletter publishers and writers do not have to pass an exam or meet any specific qualifications to promote their theories. In short, anyone can publish an investment newsletter.

So what do I do? Most investors (and brokers) don't have the time or financial resources to evaluate every newsletter. Fortunately, someone does: each February, Mark Hulbert publishes the Hulbert Guide to Financial Newsletters, which evaluates the performance of more than 100 investment newsletters. Hulbert describes each in detail and evaluates the quality and effectiveness of its recommendations according to a number of objective criteria. Hulbert also writes a regular column about the newsletter industry in *Forbes* magazine.

As you might expect, the quality of any newsletter's performance fluctuates. Only a handful consistently provide superior performance advice. Some of those that do are:

▶ *Growth Stock Outlook,* edited by Charles Allman

▶ *The Insider*

▶ *Princeton Portfolio*

▶ *The Prudent Speculator,* edited by Al Frank

▶ *Zweig Forecast,* edited by Martin Zweig

How to Make Informed Choices

Of course, newsletters are the very tip of the resource iceberg. There are scores of magazines, television programs, books, and more, if you want to take considerable time to view or read them. But the fact is, you don't need to read all those sources to make informed choices. What is necessary, however, is that you're aware of trends in the economy and business and the investment environment, so that you're capable of making judgments independent of the so-called experts. Such knowledge is important because, frankly, the opinions of experts frequently are contradictory.

Newspapers and Magazines

The most accessible source of information is the financial pages of many large newspapers. Papers vary in their coverage of financial news, so finding a good one is essential. Both *The New York Times* and *USA Today* have excellent financial sections. Many investors need to supplement their local papers with a highly focused financial paper, such as *The Wall Street Journal*, which is by far the most widely read daily financial journal. *Investor's Business Daily* also is useful, particularly if you use technical analysis.

There also are many general business periodicals and financial magazines available, such as *Business Week, Fortune,* and *Forbes. Business Week* has more news than the other two. By contrast, *Forbes* and *Fortune* (both published biweekly) focus on specific companies and business personalities. You should examine these and others, and subscribe to the one that appears most useful to you. *Barron's*, the weekly sister publication of *The Wall Street Journal*, provides a wealth of useful financial data, plus columns, features, and events significant to investors. *Money Magazine* contains many articles on investments and can be a good source of information on all aspects of investing.

If you're more statistically minded, Standard & Poor's and Moody's both publish investment information on a broad range of products. S&P's monthly is called *Stock Guide* and Moody's publishes *Outlook* and *The Standard Stock Reports* series, which are available through your broker or most large public libraries. These one-page reports provide a useful summary and description of a given firm's operations and financial history.

Probably the most comprehensive single advisory service is the *Value Line Investment Survey*, which provides a one-page summary of financial data on individual companies. It also provides rankings, on a one to five scale, of timeliness and safety. (*Timeliness* is the probable price performance relative to the market over the next 12 months; *safety* is the stock's future price stability and the company's current financial strength.) A rank of one is highest.

Online Advice

The Internet provides a king's ransom of data—from company histories and daily activity to detailed analyses of economic and industry trends, and much more.

There are many online financial databases. The best-known is *Investext*, which provides historical and current data, information on file at the SEC, market news, analysis reports, and other features. *Investext* is available from Dow Jones News/Retrieval (call 800-522-3567), from CompuServe (call 800-848-8990), or directly by subscription (call 800-662-7878). The cost is about $2 per minute, plus a per-page charge.

 Dollars & Sense: Be extremely cautious about information on the Internet. Do not mistake hot tips for valuable data.

The Prodigy online service (call 800-776-3449) offers an extensive stock data bank for a flat monthly charge, plus time charges above a certain level of usage. America Online (call 800-827-6364) and other commercial services offer stock and investment information.

LET'S REMEMBER THIS:

▶ Be careful of newsletters promising the moon.

▶ Subscribe to *The Wall Street Journal* or *Investor's Daily*.

▶ Investigate resources at your local library and try surfing—on the Internet, that is.

▼

INVESTING ON MARGIN

WHAT WE ARE GOING TO TALK ABOUT IN THIS CHAPTER:

- ▶ The Definition of Margin and How to Use It
- ▶ The Advantages and Disadvantages of Using Margin
- ▶ Tax Planning and Margin

MARGIN

One of the most widespread misunderstandings about investing in blue chip stocks is that you have to be wealthy to do it. That couldn't be more wrong. In fact, anyone can invest in blue chip stocks—you can even borrow money to do it. When you borrow money to invest, it's called *trading on margin*. Essentially, you trade on credit, using borrowed funds to supplement your own money. You make only a partial payment for the securities you buy and borrow the rest from a broker. By using borrowed funds, you can take a larger position in the stock market—that is, you can buy more shares. Borrowing the money to expand your investment opportunity for profit is called *leverage*.

A margin account is simple to open. You sign a margin agreement and a securities loan consent form, which gives the broker permission to lend the securities in your account. All securities purchased on margin are held in street name (in the name of your brokerage firm instead of your name). You do own the stock, however, and you reap the rewards or endure the losses. In addition, you get all dividends on the stock.

There are essentially three rules that govern margin trading:

1. The Federal Reserve Board's margin requirement is currently 50% (see Table 8-1). In plain English, that means you have to pay a brokerage firm at least $2,000 in cash to purchase $4,000 worth of stock. You also can deposit marginable securities in lieu of cash, also at the 50% rate. For example, if you deposit marginable securities into your account with a market value of $100,000, you are permitted to purchase an additional amount of securities totaling $100,000. Your account is then worth $200,000 ($100,000 of your money or equivalent securities plus the borrowed $100,000).

Table 8-1 Initial Margin Required (Market Value %, Effective Date)

	3/11/86	*6/8/68*	*5/6/70*	*12/6/71*	*11/24/72*	*1/3/74*
Margin Stock/ Short Sales	70	80	65	55	65	50
Convertible Bonds	50	60	50	50	50	50

As you can see in Table 8-1, not only does the margin requirement change over time, at the whim of the government, but it can be different for different types of investments.

2. Members of the NYSE are subject to stricter rules: You must have a minimum initial equity of $2,000 in cash (or stock equivalent) to open a margin account. Therefore, on a purchase of $3,000 the investor must deposit $2,000, which is $66^{2}/_{3}$% of $3,000, rather than the $1,500 required by the government.

3. Your brokerage firm may have certain requirements, among them that you have more money on the initial margin account than either the government or the NYSE require.

After you open a margin account, maintenance requirements become effective. The federal government has no regulations regarding margin maintenance, but the NYSE requires equity in the customer's account to be at least 20% of the market value of the securities held in the account. Individual firms may vary and some are higher than 20%. If the value of your securities drops below the required level, you will receive a margin call, which means you will have to add more money to the account. If you don't, your broker will sell the necessary amount of your securities to cover the call.

Dollars & Sense: Most mutual funds are marginable, just like individual stocks and bonds.

Now that you know the rules, what about the reasons. Why trade on margin? Assume you have $10,000 and you want to buy some stock. If you do so in your margin account with $10,000 in equity, you could buy $20,000 worth of stock. If your $20,000 margined stock portfolio increases in market value by 20%, thus appreciating $4,000, you would make a 40% gain on your original $10,000 equity. This is an unrealized gain in terms of tax consequences, and is, therefore, untaxed until the shares are sold. Your portfolio's market value would then be $24,000, your debit would remain unchanged at $10,000, and your equity would increase to $14,000. Your account would then have $2,000 excess equity (the amount of equity in excess of the 50% requirement). At your request, your broker could send you cash, or you could use your $2,000 excess equity to purchase an additional $4,000 worth of stock (including commissions).

One of the greatest—if not *the* greatest—reasons for investing on margin is the availability of funds. Not only does your margin account permit you to leverage stock positions, it also permits you to borrow without delay for any purpose up to your line of credit (loan value), which is based on 50% of the market value of your marginable shares.

What's more, the margin interest charged for this collateralized loan is probably the lowest percentage you could obtain anywhere. Because the collateral is always on hand, minimizing the lender's risk, margin loan rates are relatively low—generally several percentage points lower than the rates charged by banks for consumer loans and certainly much lower than credit card balance rates.

Dollars & Sense: Trading on margin is not permitted in Individual Retirement Accounts (IRAs) or other qualified retirement plan accounts.

Increased (and increasing) buying power generated by an appreciating stock portfolio can be a very important aspect of portfolio management that's not always understood by the majority of investors. For example, if you made a $10,000 purchase in your cash account (where all transactions are settled for cash by the fourth business day), and if it increased 20% in market value, you also would have a 20% unrealized gain. But you would not be able to use the gain to buy other stock unless you sold some of the shares you own to realize the gain. In other words, you would have to sell shares to raise the money for the new shares. And doing this creates a tax liability, which leaves you fewer dollars to (re)invest, at least at tax-paying time. (If you want to replace the sold shares with other shares costing the same amount, you can enter a same-day trade, but you still create a tax liability.)

Another reason to invest on margin is this: If you need cash to meet an emergency, the proceeds from any sales in a cash account are usually not available to you for four business days. The unrealized gain (along with its tax liability) and the sold stock are no longer available to appreciate further (or to decline in price, whichever the case may be).

Another reason: If you like all the stocks in your cash account portfolio and have no reason to sell any of them, you would have to choose which one to eliminate if you wanted to buy more stock and didn't have cash to pay for them. However, with a margin account you can leave your undervalued stocks alone and add other promising shares by using the buying power created by portfolio appreciation or accumulated dividends.

That's the good news. Now for the bad: There's no free lunch, especially on Wall Street. Margined or leveraged stock results cut both ways. Just as a 25% increase in the market price of a portfolio yields a 50% increase in its equity, at the 50% margined level a 25% decline in the market price would result in a 50% decline in equity at the same margined level. This leverage can lead to even greater destruction on rare occasions, such as the crash of October, 1987. You conceivably could lose all of your equity if your stock declined 50%.

Another criticism of trading on margin is the interest expense that accrues month after month, increasing your debit balance and liability. I don't buy that one either. I would willingly incur a 9% interest rate to buy something expected to appreciate 18%, for a net of 9% after interest expense gain per year. Wouldn't you? The downside of aggressively using your margin power is, even if your portfolio breaks even in terms of its market value, you might be down 1% or more. That is, if your investment hasn't increased in value, the amount of interest you're paying makes the overall return even lower. (With only half of the value of the portfolio subject to margin interest, the total percentage decline also is only half of the interest expense percentage due to the offset of dividends on the whole portfolio.)

Finally, some market observers have commented that with leverage you pay increased trading commissions that you would avoid if you bought stock with cash. I don't think this argument makes much sense: If you want to buy more shares, you'll have to pay the commission then. And to utilize the leverage of margin you must buy or sell something. To say that buying on margin increases your commission expense is like saying that making profits increases one's income tax. The truth be told, any additional commissions for additional stocks are a minor percentage of the cost basis for the stocks and of the net proceeds received from their sale. Believe me—it's worth it.

Let's Remember This:

- ▶ Borrowing money from your broker is called margin.

- ▶ Leverage can act to increase (or decrease) returns on your investment.

- ▶ Margin allows you to hold onto good performing blue chip stocks.

CHAPTER 9

WHEN TO SELL

WHAT WE ARE GOING TO TALK ABOUT IN THIS CHAPTER:

- ▶ Why You Sell Your Stocks

- ▶ Five Indicators of the Time to Sell Your Stocks

- ▶ Changing Fundamentals Can Affect Stock Prices

EVERYONE SELLS SOMETIME

Not knowing when to sell a stock (or which stock to sell) has been the frustration of many an investor, amateur and professional alike.

Imagine watching all your hard work, patience, and investment skills go down the drain with your profits, and even principal, because of one or two bad eggs. Why does this happen? It happens because the investor doesn't know when to get out of a bad situation. No one can pick winners all of the time. Even if you follow the rigid guidelines I've laid out in this book for buying blue chip stocks, there are situations that are simply unforeseeable. You will have to sell sometime—that's a given. The trick is being able to detect problems early enough to minimize the disastrous effects that a bad apple or two can have on your basket of stocks. And when you detect a problem, you must act quickly and decisively.

Unfortunately, no broker can tell you when to sell in every situation. No one can. Like each of the stocks you have analyzed in this book, brokers have their own unique stories, situations, and places in the great scheme of things. And things change—that's the nature of business and the nature of investing.

If you picked the right stocks, you'll know when to sell. That is, if you compile the necessary information about a company before you add it to your portfolio. Do that and you will quickly recognize significant changes that might indicate that it no longer meets your criteria. When that happens, it is time to sell.

Sounds pretty useless, doesn't it? I don't like the sound of it any more than you do. And so, let me share with you some of the techniques I've used over the years to manage my clients' stock portfolios.

WHEN TO SELL YOUR STOCK

Basically, there are six major indicators of when you should sell a stock:

1. The first and most important indicator of a stock gone sour is loss of revenue. If a company has a single quarter where revenues are down from the last, I sell it. The only exception to this rule is if the loss was incurred due to a one-time accounting adjustment, such as the writing off of an outdated asset or an intangible, such as good will.

Money Talks:

When a company writes off an outdated asset, it essentially declares a capital loss for that item. Because the loss is charged against revenues, revenues can artificially go down for that period, when in fact, the actual revenues without the one time charge may have gone up.

2. The companies that end up in my portfolios are extraordinarily vital and unique. They tend to have an advantage over the competition or some niche market or product. If they lose that advantage, I sell it. I quantify this fundamental change by looking at the company's market share; if it drops in two consecutive quarters, I sell it. In addition, if the company is not developing new products (that is, if expenditures on research and development are comparatively lower from period to period), I sell.

3. If a company in my portfolio has a deceleration in revenues or earnings, I sell it. It's difficult to imagine that even the best blue chip company is going to

double or triple revenues or earnings every year. I accept a slowing of revenues or earnings if it's mainly to the expanding base of those revenues or earnings. However, if I believe a company's growth rate is slowing because of a loss of it's competitive edge, it's history.

4. If the company's stock becomes overpriced, I sell it (or at least part of it). This is the hardest indicator to act on. Obviously, what seems overpriced to one person may seem cheap to another. Still, when the P/E ratios of a company get to 60, 70, or 80, or especially when they approach 100, that typically means investors have discounted the prospects of this company to the point of not making rational sense any longer. I sell companies when their P/Es get that high, even though what I want in an investment is vitality and growth. Remember, there are hundreds of good companies out there, so why place your portfolio at risk when the P/Es get suspicious?

5. When a company's stock becomes so valuable that it represents more than 10% of my portfolio, I will either sell it or sell that part of the position if the potentials are still visible. This is not because I have lost faith in it or because something is intrinsically wrong with it, but because it's begun to dominate my portfolio. It's a good stock, but I don't like exposing my portfolio to the increased risk a dominant position creates.

6. Finally, I look to various other indicators to confirm any suspicions that I might have about a stock. For example, I sell if any of the following are true:

   ▶ The company acquires an unrelated business. How many good mergers go wrong simply because they were bad marriages to begin with? You stick with what you know—that goes double for business.

   ▶ Top executives leave the firm and join the competition.

   ▶ No officers or directors are purchasing the stock. Why are the very people who are running the company and making all the decisions not buying their own firm's stock? If they won't buy it, why should I hold on to it? If they like their company, they should put their money where their mouth is.

   ▶ The company has cash left over to buy back its own shares. If a company can't or won't repurchase its own stock in the open market, something could be very wrong. Sell.

Let's Remember This:

▶ Don't fall in love with your stock. It isn't your baby; you can sell it without remorse.

▶ Sell your stocks if they show any of the following: loss of revenues; loss of niche or competitive advantage; deceleration of revenues or earnings; or P/E over 60, 70, or 80.

▶ Sell your stock if it represents more than 10% of your portfolio. Any more than that exposes you to unnecessary risk.

CHAPTER 10

▼

Black Gold: The Coming Oil Boom

What We Are Going to Talk About in This Chapter:

▶ Synchronized Economic Recovery in the Industrialized World Will Drive Up the Price of Energy Worldwide

▶ The Demand For Energy is Growing and There is No End in Sight

▶ Some Pitfalls to the Energy Boom

The Beginning of the Oil Trade

In August 1990, President Bush ordered American soldiers to Saudi Arabia to deter the military takeover by Iraq of the world's major oil exporter. As Americans sat transfixed to their televisions, the price of oil on the international market surged upwards. Gasoline prices in the U.S. soon followed. As the troops shipped out, the popular press rediscovered U.S. dependence on foreign petroleum and our resulting economic vulnerability.

During the 1970s, the American public and physicists, in particular, were bombarded by information on energy technologies, supplies, and use. The high price of oil brought about by the actions of OPEC (Organizations of Petroleum Exporting Countries) nations shocked the country into an awareness of coming shortages of fossil fuels. You might still remember seeing on television the long lines in the major cities for gasoline, particularly in Los Angeles, where cars are deeply rooted in the culture. Federal agencies and state governments financed a number of crash programs to develop energy sources and new fossil fuel development. Not much has changed in 20 years; except, of course, our growing dependence on fossil fuels.

Prior to Iraq's invasion of Kuwait, the price of oil on the international market had dropped dramatically and the energy crisis seemed to have disappeared from public consciousness. Certainly the flood of information on new energy technologies and new fuel sources, alternative and traditional, crossing the desk of nonspecialists has decreased to a trickle. Funding for energy research has also declined dramatically, along with tax incentives for energy conservation measures and the development of new energy sources.

At the same time, the public has been growing increasingly aware of the social and economic costs of unrestrained energy use. The recent rash of well-publicized oil spills and their environmental effects has raised public consciousness of the dangers of petroleum production and use. Yet oil consumption is on the rise, and the U.S. now imports at least half of the petroleum it uses. The spiraling national trade deficit raises concerns over the expense of importing large amounts of oil. The military crisis in Saudi Arabia has underscored how politically vulnerable our foreign sources of petroleum are.

So what opportunities exist in the energy sector for the astute investor? Let's explore some interesting global developments.

While the reentry of Iraq into the oil market may put some downward pressure on oil prices, the long-term trend is up at least through the next decade. Many experts are anticipating a synchronized recovery in the industrialized nations in 1997; many also believe that the emerging nations will grow at more than twice the rate of the developed countries for the foreseeable future. As developed countries enter a period of economic growth, demand for energy from both consumers and commercial users increases. From the increased use of our automobiles to massive production increases by industry fueled by new consumer spending, the demand for oil and its by-products could begin to rise rapidly.

Money Talks: The average American uses eight times as much energy as an average person anywhere else in the world. For example, there are 50 million more automobiles on the roads today versus 20 years ago. Also, today many people are driving gas-guzzling vans or trucks.

In less developed countries, like Asia, such demographic shifts as major population movements from the country to the city are placing increased demand on energy suppliers. Additionally, the huge growth in aviation in this region will drive energy demand to record highs. Engineering and construction companies and power equipment suppliers are in a position to benefit from the need for additional refinery and power-plant capacity, and the potential exists for a classic energy construction cycle to develop over the next 5 to 10 years.

LONG-TERM DEMAND FOR ENERGY

Global economic growth is the major force behind the demand for energy. As you will learn in this chapter, the globalization trends are strongly in place. The global economy will likely grow 4% in 1997 versus 2.6% in 1996. In the U.S., recent unemployment numbers have pointed to above-average growth. Japan's GDP rose at a 12.7% annualized rate in the first quarter, and loose credit conditions and weaker currencies should lead to a recovery in Europe. Investment spending and exports have accelerated in Germany and France, which represents about 40% of the European Union's total output. Developing countries that now represent 45% of the global economic picture are growing at twice the rate of the richer nations; thus they are garnering an increasing share of the global economy. By the year 2002, emerging nations will overtake the developed economies as a percentage of global economic output. Asia remains on a strong growth course and Central and South America, as well as Central Europe, are poised to rebound soon. All this growth and economic activity will require energy. The relatively low price of oil is itself a worldwide stimulus to demand.

Oil consumption is increasing more than twice as fast in the Pacific Rim as in the world as a whole. Demand for oil is growing at a 4% rate in the Pacific Rim, compared with a 1.5% to 2% rate worldwide. Much of this strength in the Far East is the direct result of urbanification, an increase in automotive transport, and a growth in aviation volume. Asia's urban population is projected to rise by more than 200 million people between 1995 and 2000, and to grow by more than one billion people over the next 20 years (see Figure 10-1).

Figure 10-1 Asia's Urban Population Boom (MM)

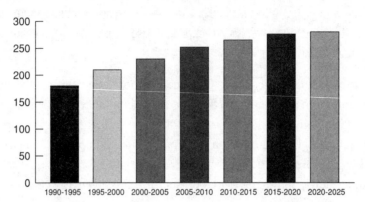

Asia's share of world oil consumption is forecast to rise from 25% currently to 30% in 2000. Given the anticipated rise in the standard of living in that region, the trend toward increased demand appears irreversible. From 71.5 million barrels per day (b/d) this year, worldwide oil demand should rise more than 5 to 6 million b/d in total by the end of this decade, or roughly 77 million b/d.

Even if the growth of the Chinese and other Far East economies slows a bit over the next five years, compared to the past five, energy consumption there will increase. The problem with demand in China has been China's lack of money, but recent trade surpluses have provided the wherewithal to buy needed energy. The expected population shift from the countryside to the cities and the rising standard of living will contribute substantially to their increasing demand. With approximately 20% of the world's population, China consumed only 3.3 million b/d last year out of a total of more than 71 million barrels. Comparing this level of per capita consumption with that of the rest of the Far East or a medium-sized third world country, the potential for economic growth in demand is staggering. There is an added stimulus to energy demand from growth in emerging economies; aging and inadequate infrastructure causes waste and inefficiency.

Take the former Soviet Union for example. Investment in infrastructure could increase the flow of oil from the Soviet Union over the long term. The implosion of the Soviet Union has been good for oil prices, but in the wake of Yeltsin's reelection, $50 billion, including $10 billion from the International Monetary Fund (IMF), is now ready to be invested in the Confederation of Independent States. A significant proportion of those funds is earmarked for investment in infrastructure, with emphasis on the oil sector. Ten years ago, the former Soviet Union produced 12 million b/d, but the obsolescence of the oil infrastructure and the poor quality of technology have reduced production to half that level. Development of the tens of billions of barrels of reserves there will be a function of capital, and $50 billion or more is now ready to be invested. However, no significant impact on the oil markets from this investment is foreseen until early in the next century.

For 1996 (through late June), spot West Texas Intermediate Crude oil prices averaged nearly $21 per barrel. Most experts had believed an average of $17.50 per barrel would prevail for 1996, increasing to $19.50 per barrel in 1997 and then to $22 per barrel by 2000. The $17.50 in 1996 has already been surpassed by more than $3.00 per barrel. Based upon the economic outlook for the U.S., Germany, Japan, and the United Kingdom, which are showing increasing signs of a simultaneous recovery beginning in late 1997, the demand for oil reflected in these price estimates could be substantially low!

Most of these countries have been pursuing easy money policies over the last few years in an effort to stimulate their economies. In the past two years, the money supply growth has been very strong in Japan, the U.S., and even Germany (more recently). These economies appear to be poised for an expansion later this year—all at about the same time! The resulting demand growth will further increase the price pressures on oil.

Add to that the current fears about inflation. In 1996, the S&P Energy Composite Index was up 6.3% versus 2.9% for the S&P 500. It was driven in part by investor's expectations of higher inflation in the next few years as the economy strengthens. If interest rates move up further, investors will no doubt flock to energy stocks.

 **Money Talks:** According to the U.S. Bureau of Labor, the cost of fuel increased 182% between 1967 and 1977. Gas and electric costs have increased 110%.

Figure 10-2 shows the relationship between the price of oil and stock performance in general. The most striking element is the very close relationship between the two. These two indices tend to move in tandem. The graph in Figure 10-2 shows the period of January 1996 through January 1997, but this relationship has been remarkably consistent throughout larger industrial periods.

Equally striking to the similarities of these two indices, are the areas of dissimilarity. What is interesting about the areas of divergence is the fact that they are not too frequent and are clearly anomalies, and the lines tend to correct towards one another almost immediately. It is this last characteristic that is very interesting to

Figure 10-2   Oil Price & Stock Performance

Current month Oil Future (left scale)

X or/ S&P 500 (right scale)

those seeking investment opportunities. Notice the divergence that exists now; stock prices are lower than oil prices. As you read in the beginning of this chapter, oil prices are going higher, which means not only must stock prices go up, but they must do so quickly and they must do so in a way to catch up with a target that is continuing to move up. Notice in the second quarter of last year when a similar divergence happened, convergence was immediate and almost ended in perfect harmony. And speaking of up, the third element you notice about this graph is that the general trend is up.

Some experts believe that the Saudis could raise production and collapse oil prices. This is unlikely because too steep a decline in oil prices would upset the Saudis' neighbors—and they don't want to start a conflict with their OPEC partners. On the other hand, oil prices could spike higher given the uncertainties and instabilities about politics in Saudi Arabia and the region as a whole. Moreover, if demand increases as I believe it will given all these factors, the development of new oil reserves will probably not keep up.

Money Talks: The world consumes one billion gallons of petroleum each day. Petroleum accounts for half of the world's energy supply.

Finally, consider this: It has been 16 years since the last peak in natural resource pricing, which historically has moved in 30-year cycles. In the early part of these cycles, investor's have made money on paper assets, but in the later stages (most recently in the 1970s when metals and chemicals did so well) it was easier to make money in real resources.

THE OIL INDUSTRY IS GREATER, LEANER, AND MEANER

After oil prices declined in the 1980s, the oil companies were forced to adopt new strategies. Whereas they previously had relied on rebounds in oil and gas prices, oil companies have taken a more conservative view of pricing in recent years. The industry has recognized that it must manage operations based on the assumption of unchanging prices, and they must do everything possible to improve profitability. The oil companies have gotten this message loud and clear and have taken it to heart. The oil companies have sold marginal operations that were too small to keep track of, they outsourced services, and they have consolidated suppliers in order to achieve economics of scale in purchasing. Mobil and Chevron, for example, could each realize $300 million in annual savings by rationalizing procurement practices. New business units have been created within most oil companies to reflect a redefinition of operations.

As you can see in Figure 10-3, over the past five years, worldwide oil industry production costs—the expense of removing the oil from the ground—have declined more than 20% to $4.29 per barrel from $5.40. Oil companies also have entered into alliances to cut costs. For example, in a major step aimed at reducing operating expenses, Mobil and British Petroleum combined their European refining and marketing operations in a joint venture with $5 billion in assets. Chevron also is realizing operating efficiencies through joint ventures, contributing its natural gas producing properties to joint operations with gas marketing companies.

The oil industry also has looked inward. Corporate culture has become less bureaucratic. The major oil companies are no longer monolithic. Layers of management have been eliminated and business units have been given more independence, making it easier for managers to get things done more efficiently. In addition, more managers' compensation is based on financial performance; whereas 10 years ago only the top managers at large oil companies were required to achieve targeted returns. With the benefits of these restructuring efforts, oil industry profits will rise 7% to 10% annually on average over the next five years. Additionally, much of this cost

Figure 10-3 Worldwide Production Costs (Dollars Per Barrel)

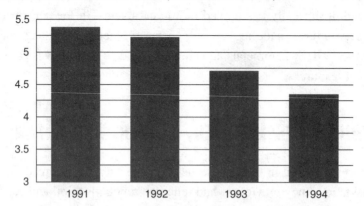

savings will be immediately reflected in dividend increases. Mobil raised its dividend aggressively in the second quarter of 1996 to $4.00 from $3.70—other major companies will follow suit. The bottom line in this: every penny of the revenue earned by the oil companies as a result of any oil price increase goes directly to their bottom line—and that is great for stock prices!

OIL AND GAS EXPLORATION AND PRODUCTION MEETS TECHNOLOGY

The need for drilling rigs has declined sharply. With 3-D seismographic technology, more exploration is done on computers. Fewer holes are drilled than in the past but the amount of oil and gas found is the same. Because of the efficiencies brought about by the use of computers, the average cost of adding reserves at the independent oil and gas exploration and production companies has declined to $4.54 per barrel from $13.50 in 1981.

Production technologies also have improved. The capability to place wellheads on the ocean floor has reduced the need for platforms, which can cost an average of $44,000 a day to operate. Flexible piping brings oil to shallow water. Drilling is now possible in areas where it was unthinkable five years ago, and more improvements are expected, as reflected in the fact that Shell Oil and Exxon have leased properties in 4,000 to 5,000 feet of water when the maximum depth for drilling today is 2,000 feet. In the last 15 years, due to hopelessly narrow margins, very few new oil drilling rigs were constructed. Now virtually all the existing drillings rigs are in service and their owners can command almost any price they want (from $29,000 per day in 1995 to $44,000 per day during the latter part of 1996, for example), and this favorable situation for these drilling companies is expected to last well into the next century.

NATURAL GAS PRICES ARE GOING HIGHER

From 1990 to 1995, overall demand for natural gas rose 17%. Environmental legislation, most significantly the Clean Air Act, has been the major contributor to the growth in natural gas consumption, which has averaged 3% annually over the last decade. Most new electrical power generating capacity has used natural gas, both at industrial companies that need to comply with the Clean Air Act and at independent power companies that have benefited from deregulation. Nuclear facilities have been almost impossible to develop, and mandated pollution control devices have raised the hurdles for investment in coal-burning plants.

In the 1990 to 1995 period, natural gas deliveries to industrial customers grew 21%, while demand increased 18% from commercial customers and 15% from electrical customers. It would not be unrealistic to expect a 2.5% increase year after year in demand to 22.2 trillion cubic feet in 1996 from 21.65 trillion cubic feet in 1995. This level of demand is close to the records of the early 1970s. However, growth is not likely to be as fast as in 1996 because of slower demand from electrical utilities due to slower growth in the economy as a whole, and some fuel switching to oil because of high gas prices.

Gas price cycles are dictated primarily by changes in supply. In 1993, the average spot price of natural gas was $1.96 per thousand cubic feet (mcf), but a spate of drilling activity pushed the average price down to $1.72 in 1994 and $1.47 in 1995. The subsequent lack of drilling has created a supply/demand imbalance that is causing prices to rise again. By 1996, the price rose to $2.10—an increase of more than 40%.

How does all this translate into opportunities for you? Well, I call it *special situation* investing. By its very definition, special situations are not the norm. That is, they exist because some significant circumstance has occurred to change the assumptions about an industry or an individual stock, which might not have been important or seemed important enough to warrant a closer look before. As you learned in Chapter 6, I don't recommend fishing from the bottom to my clients. However, special situation investing, regardless of how it appears to be similar to bottom fishing, differs specifically due to the special situation. Consequently, the structure I set forth in earlier chapters must be adhered to as much as possible, even with special situation stocks. The only real exception is that often the history of special situation stocks, for example, does not tell the full story.

Take a look at a couple of energy-related companies that would otherwise not fit into the strict buying criteria outlined for blue chips stocks in earlier chapters, but because of the major worldwide trends just discussed, will now become the diamonds-in-the-rough for the quick and well informed.

Some Stock Picks

Schlumberger Ltd. is a leading provider of drilling services and fully computerized wireline. The company has been in the doldrums for years. As you can see in Table 10-1, revenues have been in the $6 billion range, and its book value has vacillated between $13.04 and $15.16. EPS has not been stellar for the past four years, ranging from a high of $2.75 in 1992 to a low of $2.21 in 1994. Net income is almost a mirror image of EPS, and dividends during the same period managed to eke out increases from $1.20 in 1992 and 1993, rising in two consecutive years to $1.35 in 1994 and $1.50 in 1995. The dividend hikes, in my opinion, were not warranted during those years when EPS, did not increase, and quite possibly resulted from a decision made by the corporate managers solely based on the desire to put a little extra money into the pockets of shareholders to maintain their loyalty. Although Schlumberger had negative growth during the past five years and has long-term debt of $614 million with a current ratio of 1.50, it appears that they have turned their situation around when looking at these figures for 1996.

Table 10-1 The Fundamentals of Schlumberger					
Dec	EPS	REV(B)	NET(B)	BV/SH	DIV
1996	3.47	8.96	851.0	17.82	1.50
1995	2.69	7.62	649.0	14.94	1.50
1994	2.21	6.70	536.0	13.95	1.35
1993	2.40	6.71	582.0	13.54	1.20
1992	2.75	6.33	661.0	15.16	1.20
Long-Term Debt					$614,000,000
Year Growth Rate					Neg
Current Ratio					1.50

As you learned in Chapter 6, these numbers would normally make you toss this company's fact sheets in the trash—and in a hurry! But 1996 appears to be the beginning of future good times in the energy industry. As you can see in the 1996 figures, it does reflect a sizable increase in their business. Revenues grew at a 17.5% clip and earnings grew 29% during 1996, and there were healthy increases in net income to $851 million and book value per share to $17.82.

1996 is the first year of sustained earnings growth; a continuation into 1997 and beyond is anticipated in excess of 21%. Remember the old adage "earnings drive stock prices"—Schlumberger is no different, regardless of the stagnant growth in years past. In fact, the stock prices have been consistent with this lack of earnings (see Table 10-2).

Table 10-2 Four-year History of Schlumberger Stock Prices

Year	High	Low
1996	$108	$65
1995	70	50
1994	63	50
1993	68	55

Smaller companies do possess the potential to outperform the 21% growth rate of such large companies as Schlumberger. For example, Global Marine, the offshore drilling business, recently secured a five-year deep-water drilling commitment from major oil companies to drill in the Gulf of Mexico. They also have gotten two additional long-term commitments to drill in other gulf areas. As you can see in Table 10-3, Global Marine's growth rate is accelerating.

Table 10-3 The Fundamentals of Global Marine

Dec	EPS	REV(M)	NET(M)	BV/SH
1996	$1.06	$681	$180.10	$ 2.71
1995	.31	468	51.90	1.62
1994	.03	359	4.80	1.29
1993	−.17	269	−26.50	1.26
1992	.024	260	27.50	1.04

Revenues increased annually between 1992 and 1996, from $260 million to $681 million, while EPS and net income had a roller coaster ride. Both EPS and net income were probably affected by either an acquisition or a restructure change. Since 1993, things improved yearly with 1996 showing dramatic improvements in EPS, which was up some 242% on a 45% rise in revenue for the entire year.

Prospects for 1997 appear to be excellent, with higher EPS estimates averaging in the range of 70% or more. Book value per share also grew annually in the past four years, reflecting good management particularly during these difficult periods. With EPS on the increase, the possibilities of higher stock prices should follow. As of January 1997 the stock was selling at $21 and the range could be closer to $30 within 12 months. In addition to off-shore drillers, manufacturers of drilling and oil-field equipment will benefit from the coming oil boom as well.

Because of the huge demand for drilling and oil-field products brought about by worldwide population and economic changes, one of the brightest prospects for your blue chip special situation portfolio is Baker Hughes, Inc. Baker Hughes makes well head drill bits and other oil-field products, and provides oil-field services to the production industry. With nearly 90% of its total revenues derived from oilfield services, it appears to be the purest play in this strong energy production environment.

Take a look at the numbers. As you can see in Table 10-4, Baker Hughes has not seen dramatic growth in revenue, nor has the price of its stock been very exciting. Revenues increased from $2.70 billion in 1993 to $3.27 billion in 1996, while stock prices went from $29.62 to $38.87 during the same period. But management focused on improving margins, which enabled EPS to increase along with its book value per share. In 1996, EPS finally cracked through the $1.00 range, earning $1.23 versus $.67 in 1995. Estimates for 1997 appear to be in the $1.50 range and possibly could go as high as $2.00 in 1998. Book value jumped from $4.25 per share in 1993 to $6.45 per share in 1996. That's good growth and will certainly have a strong and positive effect on the price of its stock. It would not surprise me in the least to see a dividend increase sometime in 1997, if all things work out as described.

Meanwhile, revenues increased every year since 1994, as did book value. Long-term debt is relatively low and its current ratio is 2.70. If a fraction of the demographic and economic changes previously discussed translate into energy demand, Baker Hughes is poised to be one of the best performers in this industry.

Table 10-4   Current Balance Sheet of Baker Hughes

Dec	EPS	REV(B)	NET(M)	BV/SH	DIV
1996	1.23	3.27	1.76	6.45	.46
1995	.67	2.64	1.19	5.21	.46
1994	.85	2.50	1.31	4.56	.46
1993	.34	2.70	.58	4.25	.46

Long-term Debt	$674,000,000
Current Ratio	2.70

THE BEST OF TIMES, THE WORST OF TIMES

Although I believe a rebound in global growth will occur in the next few years, there are some bumps in the night that might effect this turnaround. The major disrupter of the global recovery could be the unemployment in Europe and Japan as well as in large markets, such as Mexico, Argentina, Brazil, China, Taiwan, and Russia. Real growth in many countries should emanate from the trade sector and from rising levels of private capital investments in the next few years. The drag will come from fiscal consolidation, weak personal consumption, and high levels of unemployment. Roughly one billion people, or 30% of the world's workforce, are either jobless or underemployed.

EUROPE

Among the industrialized nations, nowhere is the issue of unemployment more acute than in Europe. Roughly 18 million people, or 10.8% of the workforce, are out of work. Although a central goal of the single European market was to usher in an era of growth and jobs, nearly half of the members of the European Union are presently burdened with double-digit unemployment rates.

What's more, corporate downsizing continues to gather pace in the private sector. The privatization of state enterprises also will result in more layoffs. Meanwhile, to escape the region's high operating costs and rigid labor markets, large employers are closing plants and moving production elsewhere. So even against a 2.5% real growth next year in the European Union, unemployment may hover at 10%.

Japan

A similar situation haunts Japan. Again, a combination of weak domestic demand, corporate downsizing, and surging overseas direct investment has helped to push unemployment to 3.4%, just shy of the record 3.5% set early in 1996. Japan's true rate of unemployment is probably even higher, because many companies keep excess workers on their payrolls. The practice of lifetime employment is slowly being revamped.

The Emerging Markets

Beyond the industrialized nations, many key emerging markets confront their own labor dilemmas. Free market reforms and the embrace of capitalism in many nations have entailed wrenching policy changes, such as industry privatization, trade reform, and investment liberalization. Although the measure should pay dividends over the long term, the short-term price to pay is rising unemployment. Similarly, private-sector reforms in many nations have forced local firms to restructure and pare bloated payrolls in order to boost productivity and become competitive internationally.

In summary, a jobless global recovery carries significant risks for investors. On the other hand, with global growth poised to expand and world financial markets soaring higher, the opportunities are ripening for the astute.

Let's Remember This:

▶ Higher capital investment—not rising consumption—is likely to force global growth.

▶ Energy demand is just beginning, and there is no end in sight.

▶ Lingering high unemployment in Europe and Japan will result in loose monetary policies for the next few years.

CHAPTER 11

As the World Turns

What We Are Going to Talk About in This Chapter:

► International Trade Fuels the World

► Foreign Investors and Growing World Independence

► Profound Demographic Changes are Currently Underway

Economics, Demographics, and Interest Rates

Most of this book is devoted to describing successful techniques you can apply in your search for investments worthy of your hard-earned dollars. But when you invest those dollars in a company, you're casting a vote of confidence not only in the company itself, but also in the economy in which it must sell its products or services. In this chapter, you will learn why the American economy deserves your confidence, and why now—right now, with the 21st century just beyond the horizon—is as good an investment climate as you're likely to encounter in your lifetime. Why? Let's take a look at the global economy.

The Global Economy

First, the global economy has clearly arrived. The American economy depends on it: Exports account for more than 12% of our Gross Domestic Product, and imports account for another 13%. To put it another way, one quarter of America's economy—including all the incomes and jobs that go with it—depends on world trade. In the global economy, competitors six time zones away are potentially as serious as a competitor six blocks away. Likewise, the customer on the other side of the world plays as vital a role in a company's marketing plans as the customer across the street from corporate headquarters.

Second, America's ability to prosper in the years ahead will depend on its ability to compete successfully in the new and broadening global economy. Whether it's banks or burritos, chemicals or cosmetics, cars or computers, televisions or tractors, those companies that can do the job faster, cheaper, and better will command the marketplace.

Luckily, America is more than well-equipped to compete on a global scale.

Of course, the global economy is hardly news. Anyone who can read the name-plates on the cars on our highways and the VCRs in our living rooms already knows the world has shrunk. But the consumer's-eye view is far from complete. The list of generic products traded around the world is almost endless: Electrical materials, plywood, finished metal shapes, fish, corn, pharmaceuticals, plastic materials, industrial machinery, newsprint, and scores of other products form vast commercial linkages between nations that no nation plans to break or, indeed, can afford to break.

The volume of imports and exports involving the U.S. totals more than $1 trillion a year. And that's just products, hard goods. It doesn't include the tens of billions of dollars worth of services such as insurance, engineering, and banking. Measured in dollars, in 1992 the U.S. exported more educational services than it did corn; more financial services than wheat; more management consulting services than rice or peanuts; and more computer database services and data processing than aluminum.

International trade has been a major factor in the growth of the world's economies for the past 50 years, and especially in the past 20 years. As you can see in Figure 11-1, although the U.S. is the single largest player in the world markets, it represents only 39% of the total.

INTERNATIONAL TRADE

The international joint venture, an increasingly common characteristic of the global economy, makes partners of nations in a new and meaningfully different way. The number of joint ventures between companies in the U.S. and Japan alone is an impressive example of the growing interdependence of multinational companies.

Figure 11-1 World Market Capitalization in U.S. Dollars, as of May 31, 1996

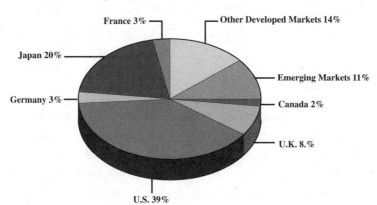

General Motors joined Toyota and Ford joined Mazda to build cars; IBM and Matsushita combined forces to build computers; Kodak and Canon signed up together to produce copiers and photographic equipment; and Boeing enlisted the high-tech help of several Japanese companies to build the Boeing 777. The advantage of this kind of cooperation is twofold. Using Boeing as an example, the company gets help financing a multi-billion dollar project and Boeing's customers get the most innovative new commercial airline in years.

Skeptical? Just look at the direct investments by different countries in the tangible assets of others. Although Japanese ownership of American businesses and real estate tends to get most of the attention, Great Britain owns as much as the Japanese do. The Netherlands, Canada, and Germany also have multi-billion dollar stakes in the American economy. The converse is also true: American companies, for their part, own more property in foreign countries than all foreign companies combined own here.

In the end, there's one string that binds together all the world's economies: money. Businesses all over the world need money to expand. They need a place to invest it and a place to park it between long-term commitments. They need a decent rate of return on it, and they need an assurance of economic stability in the place where it's being kept. In particular, these last two considerations have drawn billions and billions in foreign capital into the U.S. financial markets—winding up chiefly in bank deposits, corporate stocks and bonds, and U.S. Treasury bonds. In turn, U.S. capital plays an important role in the financial markets of other nations. Forty percent of foreign transactions involve the U.S. dollar because world traders use it as the standard measure of exchange. Forty-four percent of the world's supply of stocks and bonds is denominated in U.S. dollars, versus 15% in Deutsche marks and less than

10% in yen. Commodities all over the world are routinely priced in dollars, whatever their country of origin.

Foreign Investors

All this dealing in dollars and foreign ownership of U.S. assets worries some Americans. What if foreign investors were suddenly to pull out of U.S. markets? What if they yanked their deposits out of our banks, sold their stocks and bonds, and took their money home? Not only could these foreign investors take all their toys away, but because of the speed of electronic order taking and fund transfers, foreign investors who sold their stock and bond holdings could theoretically do so in a single day—which would be catastrophic. With billions of dollars worth of indiscriminate sell orders flooding the market and major sources of capital drying up, the value of stocks would plunge, interest rates would soar, and property values would take a dive.

Could this happen? It certainly could. One common scenario involves a fall in the value of Japanese stocks, which would theoretically force Japanese investors to sell off their U.S. holdings to cover their commitments at home. However, in 1995, Japan's Nikkei index of stocks reached a level less than half its value of several years earlier and there was no rush of Japanese investors to exit in the U.S.

On the other hand, why would foreign investors bail out in large numbers when they have such a large stake in the stocks, bonds, real estate, industrial plants, equipment, and other business property whose value would plunge, too? The more interdependent the world's economies become, the less likely it is that a foreign pullout would happen. Because the world has grown smaller, its nations have a growing interest in the prosperity of other nations. That's why the global economy is not worrisome, but good. It creates new markets and new opportunities for prosperity throughout the world.

World Interdependence

The promise of those new markets is one of the major reasons why the world is moving toward more interdependence, not less. In 1992, the Single European Act lowered trade barriers between 12 nations in Europe. In 1993, the North American Free Trade Agreement, known as NAFTA, established a trade-friendly common market for the U.S., Canada, and Mexico that will better equip North American companies to compete with a unified European market. (It's important to remember that Canada is a much bigger trading partner for the U S. than is Japan, and Mexico is our third largest trading partner.) In 1994, the world agreed to work for lower tariffs through the trade treaty known as GATT (the General Agreement on Tariffs and Trade). The nations of the Pacific-Rim (Japan, Taiwan, Korean Singapore, Indonesia, and others) need our consumer markets if they are to thrive, and we need theirs. New markets in Eastern Europe, Russia, and Central and South America lie ahead.

The efforts to build international trade bridges instead of barriers will suffer setbacks from time to time, such as the eyeball-to-eyeball confrontation between the U.S. and Japan over a threatened 100% tariff on Japanese luxury cars in 1995. But for the long run, the die is cast. The global economy is here to stay.

CAN AMERICA COMPETE?

The global economy means challenge as well as opportunity, competition as well as new markets. Can America compete? Yes. American companies are already competing successfully on many fronts, although they've lagged behind in some of the most visible areas (home electronics, for one).

A bigger question is this: Can the American economy create and sustain the kind of conditions that will lead its citizens and investors to prosperity in the global economy? Can a nation that developed the habit of spending more wealth than it created, making up the difference with borrowed money, find a way to mend its spendthrift ways?

I think so. Not because Americans have changed in any basic way in the past decade or so, but precisely because we haven't. Washington's apparent determination to deal with chronic budget deficits, as important as that is, isn't the only key to a bright future. The core of this paradox lies in significant shifts in our country's population mix. Along with the streamlining of American business that's been taking place during the past 10 or 20 years, these powerful and shifting demographic forces will constitute the most important influences on the American economy, and indeed the world, for the rest of this century and well into the next.

The Seeds are Planted

When World War I ended and soldiers returned to their wives, a profound generation was in the making. Of the 240 million people living in America today, more than 76 million were born between the years 1946 and 1964. At this writing, that generation has grown up, and the baby boomers are moving into middle age. The first of these turned 50 in 1996. Personally, they may not like the idea very much, but business economists are ecstatic over it. The aging of this massive segment of our population is expected to reverberate, mostly for the good, throughout our economy for years to come.

How? Forget the big numbers for a moment and consider the economic stages of an average person's life. In the early years, you're completely dependent on your parents for support. That ends when you finish school and start supporting yourself. You don't make much money at first, so you tend to spend it all on rent, car payments, food, clothes, and entertainment, probably relying on a lot of credit to get you through. As you move into your thirties, you're still in what might be called the acquisition phase of your life. Somehow all the money gets spent. Statistics say you've gotten married and that it takes both your income and your spouse's just to keep the household running. You're doing a lot of spending—and a lot of borrowing.

Now, multiply yourself by about 70 million and you have a pretty good idea of what was happening to the American economy for much of the 1970s and 1980s.

As you approach your mid-to-late thirties and begin to move into your forties, your priorities begin to change. You're further along in your career and making more money, but the demands on that money are different now. You've become a parent, and as the kids grow the reality of college expenses looms larger. The thought of retiring someday takes on real meaning. As a result you look for ways to save and invest the money that you used to spend as if it grew on trees. You've entered the nest egg–building years.

Again, multiply yourself by about 70 million and you have a pretty good idea of what's going to be happening to the much maligned savings rate in America over the next couple of decades.

Every seven seconds of every single day, for the next 10 years, one baby boomer will turn 50 years old. In the next 15 years, the number of people between 50 and 64 will almost double! The number of nest egg–building households headed by people between 35 and 44 years old will reach nearly 24 million by the year 2000, a growth spurt of some five million in five years. What's more, the number of households headed by people between 45 and 54 will grow by about 50% in the same period, reaching 20 million. These millions will be living and spending and saving in their peak earning years.

Households headed by 35- to 54-year-olds—those two groups just described—spend more on food, housing, clothes, and practically every other category, including financial products and services (stocks, for example) than households headed by any other age group. The households closest to the 35- to 54-year-olds in terms of their volume of spending and savings are those that bracket both sides of that age group: those headed by 55- to 64- year-olds and 25- to 34-year-olds. Both of these age groups are growing, too, and will contribute to spending and savings.

Will there be enough jobs for all these people? Where will Americans get the money to support all this spending and savings? Can the economy create enough jobs with income high enough for the new generation of middle-agers to afford to follow the pattern of past generations?

Clearly the demand will exist at home for the goods and services that American companies sell. Foreign demand also will feed the bottom line for companies prepared to compete. At the same time, demand can be expected to increase for the kinds of financial products people use to fund their college and retirement savings and investment plans.

Again, the lesson lies largely in the very population shifts described earlier. One effect of the large number of baby boomers hitting the job market in the 1970s and 1980s was a clumping up of workers at and near the entry level. This influx of inexperienced workers was responsible in part for the relatively poor productivity gains America experienced during those decades. (I say in part because the failure of American business to invest in new plants and equipment also played an important role in our relatively weak productivity growth.) Workers were plentiful—too plentiful, really, for an economy characterized by downsizing corporations—and that contributed to the problems developed in the late 1980s: sluggish wage increases and high unemployment.

As the baby boomers have aged, the pressure to generate millions and millions of entry-level jobs year after year has subsided, because the younger population groups following the baby boomers are much smaller. Baby boomers did not have as many kids as their parents, so there has been a slower growth rate in the labor force. This slower growth has helped to depress unemployment, despite continued corporate downsizing.

Social Security, which celebrated its 62nd birthday this year, will go bust just as the baby boomer population starts to retire around the year 2010. Boomers face the prospect of golden years without the helping hand of Uncle Sam because the parameter that made Social Security a viable program over 60 years ago no longer exists. In 1945, there were more than 40 workers for each Social Security beneficiary. Today, there are less than four—and the number is dropping. Thus, at today's tax rates, there simply won't be a large enough workforce to sustain the retiring generation.

A poll revealed that more people under the age of 35 believe in UFOs than in the likelihood that Social Security will be around when they retire. Even if you expect Social Security to survive in some form, you'll need to supplement it with other sources of income. History shows that blue chip stocks are your best bet.

Investor's Business Daily reported that a worker who can expect to receive $2,000 per month from Social Security when he retires could have received six times that, or $12,000 per month, if his contributions had gone into stock investments instead of going into the Social Security system. The figures assume a conservative investment strategy of 75% in blue chip stocks and 25% in smaller growth stocks. Bond investments would have provided more than $5,000 per month, also beating the Social Security system by a handsome margin.

Personal gains aside, there's the advantage to the marketplace of investing in American business, as opposed to dropping your funds down the bottomless pit known as big government. Optimists may argue that the Social Security system is cash rich. After all, Social Security collects more money than it pays out and will have a $58 billion surplus this year. The problem is that Uncle Sam raids this reserve to pay for everything from invisible Air Force bombers to food stamps.

When the Social Security coffers run dry, the solution has been to raise taxes. In 1977, Jimmy Carter implemented tax hikes and cut Social Security benefits in a reform package aimed at keeping Social Security healthy until the year 2030. But by 1983, Social Security was broke again.

CORPORATE STRENGTH IN AMERICA

Corporate America has been restructuring itself with the global economy in mind. For example, the emphasis on quality by auto manufacturers is beginning to pay off. While they still have a long way to go, U.S. manufactured cars have begun to win back buyers and regain market share.

The number of American companies that have slimmed down and reoriented them-selves to compete in the global marketplace includes many that seemed to be in big trouble only a few years ago: Xerox, which has slashed the cost of manufacturing the copier; Cummins Engine, which has doubled productivity in its plants; and Caterpil-lar, which managed to boost sales by one-third while cutting its payroll by thousands. Of course, this short list does not include American companies that never lost their stature as world leaders in their fields: Boeing, Coca-Cola, Hewlett-Packard, Merck, McDonald's, and other global giants whose names are known virtually everywhere.

As investments, companies such as these are worth investigating—that is, scruti-nizing with the criteria explained in Chapter 6. I cite them here to make the point that the rumors of America's death as a world economic power are greatly exaggerated. America is both the world's leading exporter and importer, and it's likely to remain so for many years.

THE INVESTMENT CLIMATE AHEAD

Strong companies rooted in strong economies make good investments. When you assess the forces converging in the American economy in the years ahead, the follow-ing picture emerges:

► Inflation will be relatively tame, thanks chiefly to a plentiful supply of oil that will keep energy prices in check for the entire world, and to a fierce global competition that will keep prices in check. Figure on an average inflation rate of about 3.5% per year. That's something to account for in your investment plans, but 3.5% is manageable. For comparison, inflation averaged 7.4% per year in the 1970s, 5.2% in the 1980s, and about 3.4% in the first half of the 1990s.

► Business productivity will rise as the payoff from more than a decade of reducing work forces and boosting general efficiency efforts. Despite percep-tions to the contrary, the U.S. is the world's leader in manufacturing produc-tivity. The U.S. solidified its hold on the top position in the 1980s, actually cutting labor cost while Japan's soared (when measured in terms of the dollar). This happened while productivity rose by less than 1% per year. It's expected to rise by 1.4% in the next few years. Another indicator of economic strength is that the U. S. spends more than Britain, France, Germany, Italy, and Japan combined on research and development.

▶ Interest rates will remain moderate. A slimmed-down federal deficit will reduce the government's need to borrow money in competition with business. At the same time, the increased levels of saving and investment previously described should infuse the financial markets with enough capital to finance business expansion without pushing rates up.

The bottom line, so to speak, is that our standard of living will rise as these trends take hold and the global economy provides a growing marketplace for the goods and services we want to buy and sell. This, in turn, will generate growing profits for companies that compete successfully—and for the investors who can spot them in advance. Blue chip stocks will lead the way.

Let's Remember This:

▶ The U.S. represents only 39% of the world's total capitalization.

▶ The world is shrinking and it needs money. The U.S. capital markets will help supply it.

▶ Demographic shifts in the U.S. will drive the markets for the next 15 years.

CHAPTER 12

THE TAO OF THE DOW

WHAT WE ARE GOING TO TALK ABOUT IN THIS CHAPTER:

- ▶ The Dow Theory and Its Value as a Market Predictor
- ▶ Market Bellwethers and Their Records as Predictors
- ▶ How To Use the Dow Jones Utility Index as a Predictor

THE DOW THEORY

Investors interested in buying blue chip stocks or selling them from their portfolios often rely on some methodology to help them buy or sell at the best possible time. If they don't have one already, many investors are looking for a system that can help them beat the market consistently. The method I have outlined in this book is proven; however, it is by no means the only system available. One popular alternative that has many proponents is the Dow Theory.

The *Dow Theory* is a system of market analysis developed by Charles H. Dow around the turn of the century and later refined by William Hamilton and Robert Rhea. The theory attempts to identify and measure changes in important cyclical trends in stock prices on the basis of movements in the Dow Jones Industrial Average and the Dow Jones Transportation Average.

To get a feel for the current market trend, a Dow Joneser must first establish a definite set of criteria. Unfortunately, because stock prices seldom seem to move in uniform, perfectly defined, cyclical patterns, it is difficult to develop such criteria. It is not surprising then that different Dow theorists have derived radically different criteria for Dow Theory buy and sell signals.

The common threads to most Dow Theory signals normally include the following three basic elements:

1. The industrial average and the transportation average must be doing the same thing. A signal by one of the averages but not the other is insufficient to yield a full-fledged Dow Theory signal.

2. Following a substantial market decline, a buy signal is established as follows: a rise by each of the averages to points substantially above their lows, then a decline by each of the averages of some minimum length that does not penetrate their previous lows. (Pretty murky, right? Dow Theorists have never quite agreed what the minimum should be.) Each average must rebound from this second intermediate low and establish a new cyclical recovery high.

3. Following an extended market advance, a bear market is signaled in precisely the opposite manner: a decline by each of the averages to points substantially below their major highs, then an advance by each of the averages of some minimum magnitude that does not surpass their previously established highs. (Again, the required minimum varies from one Dow Theorist to another.) Each average must decline from this second top to a new cyclical low.

Table 12-1 presents a record of major Dow Theory buy and sell signals from 1897 to 1967. Remember, this is but one of the versions of Dow Theory signals which have been developed over the years. Other analysts have used different signal parameters and have consequently derived different signal dates as well.

Table 12–1   Dow Theory Signals

Bull Markets	Bear Markets
June 28,1897–December 16, 1899	December 16, 1899–October 20, 1900
October 20, 1900–June 1, 1903	June 1, 1903–July 12, 1904
July 12, 1904–April 26, 1906	April 26, 1906–April 24, 1908
April 24, 1908–May 3, 1910	May 3, 1910–October 10, 1910
October 10, 1910–January 14, 1913	January 14, 1913–April 9, 1915

continues

Bull Markets	Bear Markets
April 9, 1915–August 28, 1917	August 28, 1917–May 13, 1918
May 13, 1918–February 5, 1920	February 5, 1920–February 6, 1922
February 6, 1922–June 20, 1923	June 20, 1923–December 7, 1923
December 7, 1923–October 23, 1929	October 23, 1929–May 24, 1933
May 24, 1933–September 7, 1937	September 7, 1937–June 23, 1938
June 23, 1938–March 31, 1939	March 31, 1939–July 17, 1939
July 17, 1939–May 13, 1940	May 13, 1940–June 15, 1944
June 15, 1944–August 27, 1946	August 27, 1946–May 14, 1948
May 14, 1948–November 9, 1948	November 9, 1948–October 2, 1950
October 2, 1950–August 31, 1953	August 31, 1953–February 4, 1954
February 4, 1954–October 1, 1956	October 1, 1956–May 2, 1958
May 2, 1958–March 3, 1960	March 3, 1960–October 10, 1961
October 10, 1961–April 26, 1962	April 26, 1962 –November 9, 1962
November 9, 1962–May 5, 1966	May 5, 1966–January 11, 1967

Source: Harvey A. Krow, *Stock Market Behavior,* Random House, 1969, p.42

The point is, the Dow Theory has been a mediocre predictor over time, regardless of which variation you use. Although many analysts have attempted to use Dow Theory for prediction purposes, it's actually better suited to identifying the present trend of the market. If the Dow Theory does have a forecasting role to play, it is in predicting the future course of the U.S. economy. It has a good record in this regard primarily because expectations of future changes in corporate earnings and general business conditions are important factors in current prices of common stock.

Dollars & Sense: You might recall that corporate earnings are the cornerstone of my blue chip system, which we discussed in Chapter 6. Earnings drive stock prices higher.

Of course, the companies contained in the industrial and transportation averages account for a very large portion of the total production and movement of goods and services in our nation's (and the world's) economy. Merging the two stock price averages into a single integrated system has long been hoped to provide an accurate stock market barometer. Primarily because of the difficulties of deriving objective signals, this new merged system is overrated.

Despite its failings, a pervasive cult has grown up around the Dow Theory over the years and many Wall Street analysts follow the theory on a continuing basis. It should come as no great surprise, then, that when a consensus Dow Theory signal attracts attention in the press, stock prices often temporarily respond to the buying or selling pressures induced by the rush of the many Dow Theory followers into the market-place. As a consequence, the theory is probably worth noting if for no other reason than to keep abreast of what the Dow Theorists are doing. On the balance, however, it is not possible to assign any significant forecasting value to the theory.

Although no work has yet been published on the subject, it is quite possible that the Dow Theory's market record could be improved by including criteria in the Dow Jones Utility Average.

Dollars & Sense: Because the utility average was first calculated in 1929, the original inventor of the Dow Theory did not have the average available for inclusion in his system.

Stock prices usually respond to sharp interest rate swings—and utility stocks are particularly interest-rate sensitive. There are two reasons for this:

► Utilities borrow large sums of money to finance plant expansion and the interest paid on such loans has a major impact on their profitability.

► Utility stocks are relatively conservative investments often purchased for their dividend yield, and they constitute an alternative investment to corporate and other bonds. Therefore, their price fluctuations closely follow those of interest-bearing securities.

Money Talks: When evaluating utility stocks, remember that their yields should be compared to bonds of similar risk quality rather than to other blue chip stocks.

Because of this dual interest-rate sensitivity, utility stocks frequently tend to lead the market prediction record. As it stands today, however, the existing Dow Theory is more of a historical curiosity as one of the earliest attempts at technical stock market analysis and less of a useful forecaster of future market trends.

WHAT ABOUT MARKET BELLWETHERS?

Investors have long searched for a stock or group of stocks whose stock prices might lead the rest of the market; these are called bellwether. If such a bellwether exists, it follows that monitoring it might give investors clues to the market's direction.

Many stocks have been suggested as possible bellwether candidates, including DuPont and Merrill Lynch. However, the only bellwether stock that has been systematically examined for predictive accuracy over many decades is General Motors.

As originally developed, the General Motors Bellwether Indicator says that when General Motors' common stock does not fall to a new low within a four-month period, the market should move higher. If General Motors fails to establish a new cyclical high within a four-month period, the market should trend downward. For example, the last buy signal shown in Table 12-2 has its roots in General Motors' December 6, 1974 low. Because it failed to go below that low by April 6, 1975, a buy signal resulted.

Table 12–2   The General Motors Bellwether Record

Date	Signal	% Gain/Loss	Cumulative Value of $10,000 Portfolio
7/21/29	Sell	+75.5	$17,552
10/30/32	Buy	+166.4	$46,758
3/9/37	Sell	+33.1	$62,245
7/31/38	Buy	+4.2	$64,859
3/12/39	Sell	+39.9	$90,764
4/18/42	Buy	+148.1	$225,185
5/29/46	Sell	+15.6	$260,269
7/16/48	Buy	+192.5	$761,288
3/14/56	Sell	+10.1	$838,483
4/18/58	Buy	+34.6	$1,128,598
11/9/59	Sell	-12.0	$993,166
4/23/61	Buy	+5.4	$1,046,797

continues

Table 12–2   The General Motors Bellwether Record [Continued]

Date	Signal	% Gain/Loss	Cumulative Value of $10,000 Portfolio
4/13/62	Sell	+19.7	$1,252,807
10/26/62	Buy	+43.0	$1,791,513
3/2/64	Sell	-20.4	$1,426,941
4/29/67	Buy	-.05	$1,419,805
1/29/68	Sell	-4.6	$1,354,353
7/29/68	Buy	+1.0	$1,367,896
2/24/69	Sell	+15.5	$1,580,057
10/26/70	Buy	+19.5	$1,888,168
8/30/71	Sell	-7.8	$1,739,947
3/13/72	Buy	+3.1	$1,793,885
8/7/72	Sell	-6.9	$1,670,645
1/21/73	Buy	-8.5	$1,528,641
5/11/73	Sell	+14.0	$1,743,262
4/15/74	Buy	-9.8	$1,570,679
7/14/74	Sell	+4.1	$1,634,919
4/6/75	Buy	+28.3	$2,098,025

The rationale behind the indicator is that as the largest industrial company in the world, what is good for General Motors is good for the market. Accordingly, trends in the price of General Motors should be able to predict the price action in all common stocks, as other companies benefit from or are hurt by the same economic forces that affect General Motors.

The General Motors Bellwether's first measured signal was on July 21, 1929, indicating that General Motors' common stock made a high four months earlier on March 21, 1929, but failed to go above that level on the upside by the signal date. General Motors continued in a downtrend until June 30, 1932, when the stock set a new low. Failing to establish yet another new low within the following four months resulted in a buy signal on October 30, 1932.

By buying and selling short in accordance with the General Motors Bellwethers signals during the last 47 years, an initial investment of $70,000 invested in the S&P composite index would have grown to $2,098,025 (excluding transaction costs), which is a compounded return of 12% per year.

By comparison, a strategy of simply buying and holding would have returned 2.3% per year, plus an annual dividend of 4%. So after commission, the General Motors Bellwether would have made a significant net contribution to your profitability. The indicator had an especially good record from 1929 through the early 1960s.

Since 1962, the record hasn't been as good. The yearly rate of return using the General Motors Bellwether strategy has been about 1%—an actual loss after commissions versus a total annual return of more than eight times that rate if you simply bought and held from 1962 to 1976. What happened?

One possible explanation is a structural problem with the assumption that the existence of a new four-month high or low is an adequate forecast of future price actions. A more reasonable explanation is that General Motors has fallen out of favor with Wall Street analysts and investors. In the 1920s and 1930s, it was a speculative favorite for investors. Therefore, it tended to attract short-term trading funds, which made it particularly sensitive as an indicator relative to speculative money. (This tends to control the psychological ups and downs of the market.) Today, General Motors is a more conservative part of a portfolio. In effect, General Motors has lost its market sensitivity.

The General Motors Bellwether ranks with Dow Theory as a historical curiosity. It is fun to follow, but it hardly rates as a profitable investment strategy.

Of course there are some stocks that have led each market run—some stock has to. But it isn't easy to find a stock that consistently leads. It is unlikely that forecasting the market will ever be done consistently.

WHAT ABOUT UTILITY STOCKS AS BELLWETHER?

As mentioned earlier, utility stocks are so sensitive to interest rates that bank and money market developments often are reflected in the Dow Jones Utility Average long before they show up on the stock market in general. For this reason, utility stocks are frequently a useful indicator of general market trends.

Money Talks: There is an inverse relationship between interest rates and bonds prices. When interest rates go up, bond prices go down, and vice versa. The easiest way to understand this relationship is to ask yourself which bond you would rather own: a bond with a 3% coupon or one with a 10% coupon. Obviously the 10% coupon is better: You would get more interest every year and, therefore, you would be more likely to pay more for that bond. Thus, as rates go up on bonds, the price of bonds with lower rates goes down.

There are several reasons for the interdependence between utility stock prices and interest rates:

▶ Owing to their customarily high dividend yield, utility stocks are often treated as a substitute for bonds, whose price fluctuations are almost totally dependent on interest rate changes.

▶ Most utilities have large amounts of debt in their capital structures, on which they must pay interest. These interest payments are critical to their profitability.

▶ The utilities depend on easy availability of funds in the capital markets to finance the expansion. Given this dependence of stock prices on interest rates, it is not surprising that utility stocks frequently change trends ahead of the general market.

Although more than 150 utility stocks are listed on the New York Stock Exchange (the largest single industry group), the 15-stock Dow Jones Utility Average (DJUA) serves as a useful proxy for our purposes of studying utilities as bellwethers.

The results of a test on the last 35 years of data reveal that if the DJUA declined during just a single week, the chance that the general market would rise in the following six months was about 60%. If the DJUA rose during one week, the probability of a subsequent market rise increased to 76%. Statistically the difference is very important, because the average probability of a market rise over any six-month period is about 66%.

In other words, the mere knowledge of a DJUA advance or decline in one week provided information on the future trend direction of the market. Of course, an examination of week-to-week changes is extremely crude and signals are subject to whipsaws.

One solution is to compare the current DJUA level to the level of 15 weeks earlier. If the present reading is higher, utility stocks may be classified as being in an uptrend and the stock market should follow upward as well. If the current DJUA is lower, a downtrend is indicated and the broad market should follow the utilities lower. Because the DJUA has a greater chance of moving in one direction or the other over a 15-week period than in a single week, buy and sell signals are less frequent and whipsawing is reduced. Used in conjunction with other indicators, such as those previously discussed, this analytical technique can help predict the market trends.

Another system of analysis that has proven effective uses a comparison of the current DJUA reading with the average weekly value of the index over the past year. Depending on whether the present reading is above or below the one-year average, the market is deemed to be bullish or bearish. This method tracks market trends extremely well and is even less subject to whipsaws, although it is not as sensitive in picking up market turning points as the two previously mentioned.

The utility stock average provides a unique money-sensitive measure of investor sentiment. It is a valuable leading indicator of the market's future trend.

NEWS AND THE MARKET

You have probably picked up the newspaper, turned to the financial section and seen headlines declaring "Market Rallies on Good Earnings News" or "Explosion Socks it to Markets." It would seem there is a specific reason behind every day's market action or at least journalists think so. Are the headlines true? Does the news affect the markets in a specific way or does this just reflect the newspaper's need to sell the next day's paper? The role that news does play in market fluctuations is debatable.

Several studies have reached widely varying conclusions. Most of the analyses on this subject have been plagued with natural biases. Just what does constitute good or bad news for the stock market? This is frequently a matter of subjective judgement or interpretation. For example, is news of rapid money supply growth good because it increases financial liquidity, thereby enabling people to buy stocks? Or is it bad because it ultimately heats up inflationary pressures and therefore destroys investor confidence?

There is another dangerous bias involved in already knowing subsequent market performances and unconscientiously using that knowledge as the basis for describing certain news events as good or bad. The news of each day is a mixture of good and bad. If the market rises, it will be attributed to a favorable item of news, with the next morning's paper often noting that traders ignored this or that unfavorable development.

The stock market is relatively efficient in responding rapidly to obviously significant news events and in adjusting prices to reflect updated knowledge. Three factors generally determine the impact an event will have on stock prices:

1. Its financial earnings, dividend payout, and so on. Obviously the more pervasive and extreme the news impact, the greater its effect on market prices.

2. The extent to which the event deviates from market expectations is critical. A fully expected event by definition is not news, and will not appreciably affect stock prices. But if an event is not expected to occur, or at least is not widely expected to occur, and it changes the future earnings and dividend prospects of a stock or the market, then prices should react accordingly.

3. Finally, the more efficient the market mechanism, the quicker the price adjustment.

The bad news about news is this: With the expectation of those events that the public and market analysts have traditionally misunderstood or failed to understand at all, such as complex Federal Reserve System actions, or which have gone relatively unnoticed and hence unappreciated, the U.S. stock market has invariably responded too quickly to allow most investors to profit from them.

In general, extremely bad news events outnumber extremely goods news events. Bad news tends to follow bad news, and good news tends to follow good news. In general, acting on news events has rarely been a profitable endeavor. A well-informed investor who has developed a rational set of expectations about the direction of the market will unlikely improve that position based on the latest news story.

A Unified Theory of Prediction

Complex problems rarely have simple solutions, yet simplicity is the routine most investors are seeking. The following are the three most common simplistic solutions to market forecasting:

1. That which has happened will continue to happen;

2. The forecasting game cannot be won so there is no use in trying; and

3. The market is so inefficient that virtually any system of forecasting will work.

All of these are wrong; yet they seem to be somehow related to an integrated system of market prediction. However, before these and any other indicators can be integrated, a general rational theory of market behavior must be agreed upon.

The theory underlying stock market fluctuations is quite elementary. In a continuous auction market, supply and demand are always precisely equal. When you hear that the markets were hit with a flood of panic selling, usually what is ignored is the elementary fact that every share sold is purchased by someone. Conversely, when waves of profit taking hit the markets, the markets don't collapse because for each profit taken there is a profit seeker. That is, every stock sold is contemporaneously bought.

The ability to foresee and profit from future price changes in the stock market rests on one's ability to:

▶ Assimilate, correctly interpret, and act on available information before it is fully appreciated by most market participants. Although most information is disseminated almost instantly, it is assimilated slowly and understood by a small portion of the investing public.

▶ Measure the mood of the market participants. Most investors buy stock because they expect the price will go up; most investors sell stock because they believe the price will go down. These expectations drive the fluctuations in the markets.

LET'S REMEMBER THIS:

▶ The Dow Theory is a good barometer of the U.S. economy, but is not particularly useful as a market predictor.

▶ General Motors has lost its usefulness as a market bellwether.

▶ The Dow Jones Utility Average has a good track record as a market predictor.

▼

CONTRARIAN: TO BE OR NOT TO BE

WHAT WE ARE GOING TO TALK ABOUT IN THIS CHAPTER:

► What is a Contrarian?

► The Potentials and Limitations of Market Timing

► What is Index Investing?

CONTRARIAN THEORY

The investment strategy I have outlined throughout this book has proven itself time and time again. But it is by no means the only strategy available. You just learned about the Dow Theory and how to use market bellwethers. Now take a look at a few other theories.

A *contrarian*, as the name implies, goes the opposite way the crowds go. I suppose the professional contrarian would object to this description, as it might imply some mental or physical problem. But the fact is, contrarian investors are quite sane, and very strongly opinionated about their theories. They capitalize on the aspect of market behavior that's psychological, but that's not to say there isn't a financially logical reason for going against the crowd.

You see, stock prices follow the laws of supply and demand: When demand increases, the price rises. But there's only so much stock and so much money to buy it. Therefore, as more investors act on their anticipation that a stock is going to go up, more purchasing power is used up, which means the market for that stock is closer to its peak. Conversely, when investors sell, there's more cash to create upward pressure on a stock, representing an opportunity.

That's the theoretical rationale for contrarianism. To the contrarian, if it's true that the crowd always buys high and sells low, it's also true that the crowd almost invariably overreacts to news—both good and bad. The difference between real and perceived risk is opportunity. This is an essential part to every contrarian theory.

Of course, there are contrarians and then there are contrarians. Everybody wants to buy low and sell high, but a true contrarian's actions are contrary to conventional wisdom. That is, a contrarian must act against his own human nature. Most people, investment professionals included, cannot do this. It seems un-American to want the economy and/or the stock market to tank.

The majority of professional contrarians take their cue from more courageous contrarians and wind up simply following a different crowd. In practical terms, that just means they sell somewhere along the way up and buy somewhere along the way down. Just like many investors, professional contrarian investors as a group are no exception to our rule—and most of them don't beat the market.

MARKET TIMING

Market timers use technical analysis of historical price performance to try to predict future movements. In effect, they say, "Forget the facts, show me the chart." They use statistics and are guided by historical chart patterns, known by such names as head and shoulder, double tops, triangles, gaps, and rising bottoms.

Cycles of various sorts are a fact of market life, and always have been. There are seasonal and other historical market patterns that have a logical basis and recur with phenomenal consistency. But the past isn't necessarily a prologue, and history rarely repeats itself exactly. Investors who use a market timing approach exclusively have about the same record of beating the averages as other professionals.

Still, market timing techniques can have some validity, and the investor who doesn't make a point of becoming familiar with the techniques is missing out on an opportunity to enhance returns.

I want to emphasize that to underperform the market is not necessarily to lose money. In fairness to many professionals, most managers of equity portfolios who have applied a consistent approach with discipline, whatever that approach is, have made money for their clients over the long term when they haven't beaten the averages. Indeed they should have, because the market has risen over the long term. However, there are significant limitations to market timing techniques. Specifically, what if you're wrong? I know, I know, you will be right. Right? Humor me on this one. Take a look at the market period from 1980–1989 (see Table 13-1).

Table 13-1 The Value of Staying Invested 1980-1989

Percent Invested	In	Out	Return
100%	2,528	In All Trading Days	17.5%
99.6%	2,518	Out 10 Best Days	12.6%
99.2%	2,508	Out 20 Best Days	9.3%
98.9%	2,498	Out 30 Best Days	6.5%
98.2%	2,488	Out 40 Best Days	3.9%

Return based on S & P 500 Index

During that time period, the market provided an annual average return of 17.5%. Not too shabby. Most of those gains were made during only 40 days of the total 2,528 days that the market was open. If you managed to miss all 40 of those days (that is, if you had your money on the sidelines waiting to time the markets rather than invest in the S&P 500 Index), you would have earned a stellar 4% on your money! That means if you missed only 40 days—granted they were the key days, but you didn't know that then—your $10,000 would have grown to $14,802. Had you done nothing—no timing whatsoever—your $10,000 would have grown to $50,591!

Okay, so you're not that bad at market timing, you say?

Say you only missed the 20 best days. You did 50% better than the first example—your return dropped from 17.5% to 9.3%.

Now for another example. Suppose you, like thousands of others, want to buy at the very bottom of the market every single year, and say you somehow did that for 20 consecutive years, from 1971 to 1990. During that period, you invested $5,000 each year at the absolute best possible time that year. Your average return over that 20-year period would have been 16.5%. Very good.

Now, suppose you're as dumb as a post, or at least terribly unlucky, and you invested $5,000 each year for the same period, but this time you managed to buy at the peak of the market each year. Your return would have been 14.8%. Figure 13-1 shows that poor timing of the market makes your high-performing stock portfolio no better than a poorly performing Treasury bill portfolio. The point is, timing, although it can enhance your return, can expose your portfolio to substantial added risks.

Figure 13-1   Market Returns 1945-1989
(Stock minus 40 best months of 540 months)

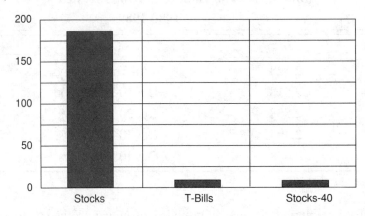

Although there will be years when the stock portfolios show losses rather than gains, the importance of avoiding losses—and the professionals who cause them—can't be overstated. Imagine making money for a few years, then seeing it wiped out because somebody did something stupid. It's an arresting fact that to overcome a 50% portfolio loss, you need a 100% gain.

Unless you're Ivan Boesky, it's impossible to predict with certainty what a stock or the stock market is going to do in the short term. That's why discipline and patience are essential ingredients for successful investing.

The Professional Dilemma

There are more reasons why most money managers fail to match, let alone beat, the Dow or the S&P 500. These reasons are worth looking at because there are traps that you, as an individual investor, can avoid.

In 1995, 80% of all mutual fund managers underperformed the S&P 500 Index and in 1996, 76% of all fund managers underperformed the S&P 500 Index.

One reason is the short-term focus that most investment professionals have developed in the past 20 years. Such factors as deregulation of the financial markets, rising personal incomes, a long-running bull market, IRAs, and other tax legislation worked to change the investment markets in two fundamental ways:

1. Personal investing, formerly the province of the wealthy, was brought within the reach of just about anyone. That was a welcomed development, but it vastly increased the market for investment services.

2. The financial service industry, consisting of a dizzying assortment of investment professionals, including mutual funds, independent money managers, banks and insurance companies, financial planners, and stockbrokers, began competing for investors' hard-earned dollars.

It's hardly surprising that the one who provides the best long-term investment returns through patience and discipline isn't the one who makes the headlines. The pressures that the marketplace puts on mutual funds to produce quarterly performance is unbelievable. The result, more often that not, has been short-term portfolio profits at the expense of higher long-term returns. That and a self-defeating attempt by investors to go with the hottest fund or money manager, make buying high and selling low a virtual certainty.

Another important factor contributing to a short-term focus has been the need to provide liquidity. A mutual fund, for example, must be able to meet shareholder redemptions if necessary, possibly in big numbers should the market decline or the fund's performance turn sour. This required flexibility means mutual funds must hold stocks that can be gotten in and out of with relative ease—namely, the largest companies with the largest number of shares outstanding. Not only do these high-cap stocks tend to be mature companies with less potential for sales-driven growth than younger, smaller-cap firms, but when a lot of huge institutional investors jam into relatively few large stocks, the result is less flexibility, not more. For example, you can't, with care, dump a whole position in General Motors on the market. It has to be done over time. Lack of flexibility results in lower returns.

Dollars & Sense: The liquidity factor in mutual funds is often sighted as one of the main reasons why investors get higher returns from loaded funds—that is, mutual funds that charge an up-front fee or some declining exist fees to purchase and/or sell these shares—than investors in no-load funds. The simple human reaction to not want to incur these charges keeps people from bailing out of the loaded funds in bad times. Consequently, these investors make more money, because they are not sitting on the sidelines when the markets turn around.

The problem a quarterly mentality brings to stock investing is not a lack of short-term opportunities, which exist in abundance even among the largest stocks. The problem is that investors forced into such a tight time frame are forced to take short-term losses along with their short-term gains and often have to forgo better returns that could be had by following a more disciplined approach.

As a personal investor free of institutional investors' constrictions, you have the best of both worlds: the opportunity to capitalize on relatively short-term price increases and the ability to follow a system that increases your odds that you will be buying low and selling high.

Professionals who actively trade and follow a lot of stocks also have high overhead. In addition to management fees (typically 1%), there are transaction costs, custodial fees, and other legal and administrative expenses that take their toll, so even portfolios that match the market in terms of pure performance underperform in net returns to their clients.

There's one other reason most professionals underperform: They simply make the process too complicated.

Part of the reason they make it complicated is that they have to. Either they are required by law to be widely diversified, as with mutual funds, or they feel extensive diversification is necessary to avoid criticism—or even lawsuits, should one of their heavy positions take a beating. Overdiversification can dramatically inhibit better-than-average profits due to the fact that many stocks, as a group, must perform well. Usually this is not the case.

And then there are egos. How can you look like a genius if what you're doing isn't complicated? And there's the need to justify fees. How can an investment manager accept a percentage of the assets unless he or she looks busy? And still another part of it is simply human nature. Remember O'Higgin's Law? If it's important—and money always is—we can't resist making it complicated.

INDEX INVESTING

Because most mutual funds and independent money mangers fail to beat the averages, one way of outperforming the pros is to buy the averages. If you can't beat 'em, join 'em. To do this, buy one of a number of mutual funds that replicate indexes, such as the AMEX Major Market Index (an index of 20 stocks designed to correlate with the Dow), the S&P 500, the New York Stock Exchange Composite Index, or the Value Line Composite Index.

These funds simply buy and hold the stocks making up the index or a representative sampling thereof. One example of an index fund that replicates the S&P 500 is the no-load Vanguard 500, which has no management fee and a very low expense ratio. Other index funds have nominal management fees.

Although expenses, however minimal, cause stock index funds slightly to underperform the market as they represent it, they nonetheless outperform some 75% of all general stock funds and money managers. The most persuasive supporters of such passive investing are advocates of the *efficient market hypothesis*, also known as the *random walk theory*. Its practitioners contend that past, present, and future stock prices over a broad spectrum simply reflect information coming into the market at random. Thus, while there may be investors who overachieve and those who underachieve, over the long haul there is no knowledge or judgment an investor can add beyond what has already been perceived and reflected in prices.

In the words of Burton Malkiel, whose *Random Walk Down Wall Street* advocates passive investing, "a blindfolded chimpanzee throwing darts at a *Wall Street Journal* can perform as well as the experts." Hence money spent on active portfolio management, including management fees and transaction costs, is money ultimately wasted, and the relatively small cost of passive investing is well justified.

The efficient market hypothesis has its staunch supporters and many detractors. The fact that the S&P 500 significantly underperformed active managers from the mid-1970s through 1982 is cited as hard evidence among investment professionals who consider the theory academic nonsense. Proponents argue that the market's information processing and pricing mechanisms were less efficient in the 1970s than in the 1980s, when computers became more widely used in the securities marketplace dominated by large institutions.

A final word on indexing: The most effective argument against indexing is that while you do no worse than the market, you do no better, either. After all, you can do as well as the market and still go broke.

The Dogs of the Dow

When seeking above-average growth potential over the long run, simple investment strategies can sometimes be the most effective. Successful stock market investors usually follow disciplined investment philosophies, such as the following:

▶ Buy quality

▶ Invest for the long term

▶ Stick with a discipline

▶ Refresh your portfolio systematically

Consider one alternate investment strategy that employs this philosophy in an attempt to outperform the Dow. This strategy focuses on dividends and low price. This blue chip strategy entails the following steps:

1. Calculate and rank the dividend yield on each of the 30 companies in the Dow (annual dividend divided by stock price).

2. Identify the 10 with the highest dividend yield and buy equal amounts of each.

3. Hold them for a period of one year—do not make even a single trade, no matter how ugly it gets.

4. At the end of that year, adjust the portfolio to include the then-current group of the 10 highest-yielding stocks.

This simple strategy would have yielded a higher total return to you than an investment in the Dow. For example, in the year ending September 30, 1995, the Dow yielded a total return of 27.57%. This strategy for the same time period returned 30.79%. In 1994, the Dow returned 10.97%; this strategy returned 14.44%. If you average the returns over time, the comparison is even more dramatic (see Table 13-2).

Table 13-2 The Dow 10 versus the Dow 30					
Average	*3 years*	*5 years*	*10 years*	*20 years*	*25 years*
Dow 10	24.23%	21.31%	19.33%	16.56%	15.76%
Dow 30	21.11%	17.26%	16.21%	13.87%	12.39%

So beating the Dow by 13% to 27% annually isn't enough for you? Try this little modification to the strategy:

1. Again, rank the 30 companies in the Dow by dividend yields.

2. Pick out the top 10 dividend yielders.

3. This time, buy only the five lowest priced of that 10.

4. Again, hold them for better or worse for one year and then readjust.

Had you done this for the past 3, 5, and 10 years, you would have picked up, on average, an additional 8.57%, 10.71%, and 6.00% over the Dow 30 (see Table 13-3).

Table 13-3	The Flying Five versus the Dow 30				
Average	*3 years*	*5 years*	*10 years*	*15 years*	*25 years*
Flying Five	29.68%	27.97%	22.21%	16.65%	15.97%
The Dow 30	21.11%	17.26%	16.21%	13.87%	12.39%

This investment approach of buying companies with high dividends relative to their share prices is designed to increase the potential for higher total returns. Because a stock's dividend yield is a reflection of its price, as the price goes down the yield goes up. Focusing on these high dividend-yielding blue chip stocks is one way of identifying companies whose stock prices may be currently undervalued or depressed. Of course, this defies conventional wisdom as well as doing the one thing I discourage, bottom fishing. But, if you want to diversify and use a valid contrarian idea, then go for it!

The great thing about these two contrarian strategies is that they tend to do well in sideways or down markets, yet give up very little in raging bull markets. These shares tend to do better in bad markets because they are already relatively undervalued (as measured by a high dividend yield) and thus don't have as far to fall. Additionally, their dividends help support the share price. In 1973 and 1974, for example, the steepest and largest bear market in post-war history, the flying five posted a 15.8% gain and the Dow 10 managed a 7.6% increase. Meanwhile, the Dow posted a heart-stopping 36.2% loss.

In 23 years, the flying five has lost money only twice, though it has under-performed the Dow four times. The Dow 10 has lingered in negative territory three years and has underperformed the Dow five times. The only exception to that rule was in 1990, the year of the Gulf War: The Dow dropped just 0.4%, but the flying five plunged 15.2% and the Dow 10 dropped 7.6%. But the very next year, the two strategies bounced back. The flying five soared by nearly 62% and the Dow 10 increased by nearly 40%. The Dow jumped only 24%.

LET'S REMEMBER THIS:

► Contrarians like out-of-favor stocks.

► Trying to time the markets is a waste of time. Discipline and patience are the keys to successful investing.

► Most professional managers have a short-term focus.

PORTFOLIO SMARTS

WHAT WE ARE GOING TO TALK ABOUT IN THIS CHAPTER:

▶ What is Asset Allocation?

▶ How Can it Impact Your Returns?

▶ The Assets You Should Include in Your Portfolio and Why

ASSET ALLOCATION

I have talked a great deal about specific blue chip stock strategies. But stocks should only represent one part of your diversified portfolio. Now I'll turn to the remaining part of the portfolio and how to properly diversify.

In the early 1960s, the term *asset allocation* did not even exist. The traditional view of diversification was simply to avoid putting all your eggs in one basket. The argument was that if all your money was placed in one investment, your possibilities ranged from winning big to losing big. Alternately, by spreading money among a number of different investments, the likelihood was that you would not be right on all of them or wrong on all of them at the same time. There is an advantage, therefore, in having a narrower range of outcomes.

In the 1960s, individual investors owned several dozen stocks and bonds with some cash reserves. Because the U.S. stock and bond markets constituted the major portion of the world capital markets, most investors did not even consider international investing. It was during this period that the U.S. government followed the Keynesian Theory of economic management. Named after the economist John Maynard Keynes, the theory called for manipulation of the economy by controlling the amount of government spending. Under this scenario, the government fixed interest rates. Consequently, fixed income investments, such as bonds, were relatively stable, conservative investments. What's more, because the interest rate was set above the level of inflation, the return on these kinds of investments was quite adequate. Bonds traded in a very narrow price range, which is no longer true (see Table 14-1). Security analysis activity, therefore, focused more on common stocks where the payoff seemed greatest for superior investment skill. The majority of transactions on capital market exchanges were noninstitutional. That is, most trades were done by you and me, so it was commonly believed that a full-time skilled professional should be able to beat the market consistently.

Table 14-1   Changes in Standard Deviation of Long-term U.S. Government Bonds

	1960s	*1986-1991*	*1991-1995*
Long Term U. S. Government Bonds	2.5	12.6	8.9

Later, during the late 1970s and early 1980s, the government changed its operating procedure from the Keynesian Theory to the Monetarist Theory. The Monetarists believed that the way to regulate the economy was to control the money supply rather than to control government spending. Under this system, interest rates were allowed to move freely in response to market conditions. With the passage of time, bonds moved out of their narrow trading ranges while price volatility increased dramatically due to large swings in interest rates. As you can see in Table 14-1, the risk associated with the long-term U.S. government bond, as measured by standard deviation, has increased since the 1960s. (See Appendix C for a full definition and description of standard deviation.) This means that bonds are no longer a safe haven for the conservative investor. In fact, bond prices can gyrate dramatically—much like stock prices. During this period another important change occurred: Institutional trading on the exchanges increased to more than 80% of all activity. This means the average investor is now competing against well-educated, well-paid financial experts, rather than the local grocer or barber.

Imagine for a moment the floor of today's New York Stock Exchange: Millions of transactions are occurring between willing buyers and sellers. Around any single transaction, there is a fundamental competition. The buyer has concluded that the security is worth more than the money, while the seller has concluded that the money is worth more than the security. Both parties are now likely to be institutions that have nearly instantaneous access to all publicly available relevant information concerning the value of the security. Each has very talented, well-educated investment analysts who have carefully evaluated this information and have reached opposite conclusions, that is, one wants to buy and one wants to sell. At the moment of the trade, both parties are acting from a position of informed conviction; they each believe they are right. Because of the dynamics of a free market, their transaction price equates supply with demand for the security. The current market price, therefore, is a price that reflects the security's intrinsic value. (If not, either the buyer would not buy, or the seller would not sell.) This is the result of an efficient marketplace.

MODERN PORTFOLIO THEORY

Most research evidence supports the notion that the markets are reasonably efficient. Accelerating advances in information processing technologies will undoubtedly drive the markets to even greater efficiency in the future. It thus becomes even more unlikely that anyone will be able to beat the market all the time.

Modern portfolio theory has as its foundation the notion of efficient markets. As this body of knowledge developed, the focus of attention shifted from individual securities to a consideration of the portfolio as a whole. Modern portfolio theory, therefore, redefined the notion of diversification. It went far beyond the idea of using a large number of baskets in which to carry one's eggs. Indeed, major emphasis was placed on finding baskets that were distinctly different from one another. That was important because each basket's unique pattern of returns partially offset the others, with the effect of smoothing overall portfolio volatility. When one asset is up, another might be down, and vice versa. The overall return would be somewhere in the middle.

The graph in Figure 14-1 shows the market value of two different assets over time. Investment A swings up and down with market activity, economic cycles, and political changes over time. Investment B also follows its cycle reacting to those same forces. What is interesting about these two assets is that they tend to react to the marketplace in opposite directions. They are said to have a negative correlation. (See Appendix D for a definition and description of correlation coefficient.) That is, when one asset goes up, the other goes down.

Figure 14-1 Benefits of Diversification

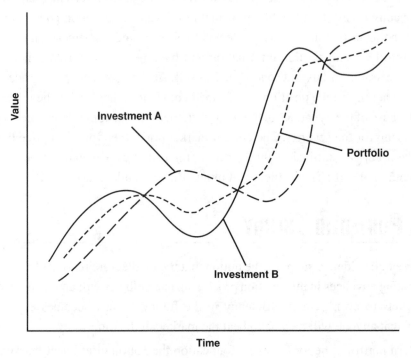

Money Talks: Asset classes are, by definition, somewhat negatively correlated because each asset class is a group of securities whose performance in the marketplace is similar to each other and dissimilar to all others.

With a portfolio mix that uses both assets, an investor smoothes out the ups and downs of the market and earns a return somewhere in the middle. It is this combination of differing assets that makes asset allocation so powerful.

Today's investment world is very different from that of the past. The number and variety of investment alternatives have increased dramatically, and once-well-defined boundaries between asset categories often overlap one another. We now deal in a global marketplace in which America's share of the world capital markets has shrunk to a minority position. Computer technology delivers relevant new information regarding a multitude of investment alternatives almost instantaneously to a market-place, and that marketplace is dominated by institutional investors. For these and other reasons, the traditionally diversified domestic stock and bond portfolio is clearly inadequate in today's investment environment. Enter the concept of asset allocation.

ASSET ALLOCATION

Asset allocation is a way of building a stronger portfolio that, of course, includes blue chip stocks. Designing an investment portfolio consists of several steps:

1. Decide which asset categories will be represented in the portfolio.

2. Determine the long-term target percentage of the portfolio to allocate to each of these asset categories.

3. Specify for each asset category the range within which the allocation can be altered in an attempt to exploit better performance possibilities from one asset category to another.

4. Select securities within each of the asset categories.

Steps 1 and 2 form the foundation for portfolio risk/return characteristics and often are referred to as *investment policy decisions*. Traditionally, a diversified portfolio was built with three asset categories: cash equivalents, bonds, and common stocks. However, other asset categories, such as international bonds, international common stocks, real estate, and precious metals, must be considered. To the extent to which these asset categories are affected differently by changing economic events, each will also have its own unique pattern of returns. The capability of one asset category's pattern of returns to partially offset another's is the key to the power of diversification in reducing portfolio risk. Imagine the graph in Figure 14-1 with eight lines instead of two. The action of these asset groups, whose vary nature differs from one another, creates a situation where such a portfolio would ride smoothly through every economic condition, and that ride would be completely predictable. (See Appendix E for a complete description and analysis of the model portfolio.)

When considering which asset categories to include in your portfolio, begin with the premise that all major asset categories will be represented unless specific sound reasons can be established for the exclusion of one or more of them.

Wise asset allocation suggests that in an efficient market, an investor of average risk tolerances should maintain a portfolio that mirrors the proportions in which the world's wealth is allocated among the various asset categories. As you can see in Figure 14-2, all the assets of the world can be generally classified into these eight classes, only seven of which are considered investment classes (because cash is not an investment). In addition, venture capital is too speculative for the purposes of investing, so it is not considered an asset group for this purpose. So, if you gathered all of the world's assets and placed them in categories, everything would fit into the following seven classes:

1. Domestic bonds

2. International bonds

3. Blue chip stocks

4. Small capitalization stocks

5. International stocks

6. Real estate

7. Special assets (precious metals, commodities, collectables, and so on)

Of course, there are more specific categories, but they are all subsets of these general classes. The rationale being: If the world's money is invested like this, as it shows in Figure 14-2, there must be a good reason.

Figure 14-2 Total Investable Capital Markets as of December 31, 1988

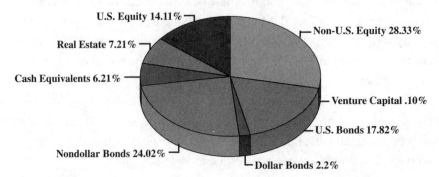

Active security selection is predicated on the belief that exploitable inefficiencies exist at the individual security level, inefficiencies that can be identified through skilled analysis. To add value to a portfolio, a manager must produce an incremental return in excess of the transaction costs and associated fees—a difficult, although not necessarily impossible achievement in an efficient marketplace.

Money Talks:

In 1995, more than 80% of all fund managers underperformed the S&P 500 Index. In 1996, more than 76% of all fund managers underperformed the S&P 500 Index.

Dramatic support of the importance of asset allocation is provided by a study of 91 large pension plans covering the period of 1974 through 1983 ("Determinants of Portfolio Performance II: An Update," by Gary P. Brinson, Brian D. Singer, and Gilbert L. Beebower, in the *Financial Analysts Journal,* May–June). The Brinson, Singer, and Beebower study sought to attribute the variation of total returns among the plans to three factors: asset allocation, market timing, and security selection. In other words, they wanted to know why one portfolio performed better than another. So they looked at large pension plans, each managed by professional managers that had staffs of analysts, and so on.

They looked at the portfolio manager's ability to pick stocks: They wanted to see whether these managers were able to find winners and avoid losers consistently. They then analyzed the portfolio manager's ability to time the markets. Did these managers move money into the markets at the bottom of a swing and move money out of the markets at the peaks? Next, they looked at the portfolio manager's investment policy— that is, the asset allocation model they used: how much money should be in stocks, how much in bonds, how much in real estate, and so on. The study concluded that on average a startling 93.6% of the variation could be explained by the asset allocation policy followed. Market timing, in conjunction with asset allocation policy, explained 95.3% of the variation in total returns among the plans. Similarly, 97.8% of the variation in total returns among the plans was explained by the combination of asset allocation with security selection. To summarize, the return in your portfolio will largely be determined by your asset choices and their relative size in your portfolio. Market timing and security selection will barely impact your overall return.

Figure 14-3   Determinants of Portfolio Performance

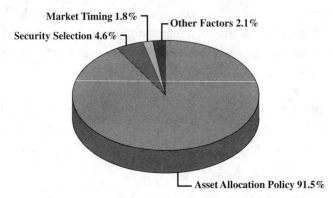

The Brinson, Singer, and Beebower study clearly supports the notion that asset allocation policy is the primary determinant of investment performance (see Figure 14-3), with market timing and security selection both playing a relatively minor role.

These strategies do not fight the capital markets as much as they intelligently ride with them. With a properly diversified portfolio, you can focus your investment decision on specific investments within each category. As for stocks, you have the tools to substantially increase your performance.

Let's Remember This:

▶ Diversify among different investments.

▶ Institutions now dominate the market.

▶ Your selections of investment categories, that is, your asset allocation decision, is the most important determinant of your portfolio's performance.

▼

THE COMMITMENT AND THE TEMPTATION

WHAT WE ARE GOING TO TALK ABOUT IN THIS CHAPTER:

▶ Recap Investment Philosophy

▶ How to Avoid Investment Distractions

▶ Sticking With Your Plan

Managing your investments is simple, but not easy. It is simple because successful investing principles are relatively few in number and easy to understand.

One such principle—the most important—is the weighing of risk. Although all investors face several risks, the two most important ones, as discussed in Chapter 2, are inflation and the volatility of returns. The more a portfolio is structured to avoid one of these risks, the more it unfortunately becomes exposed to the other. Therefore, you must determine which risk is more dangerous to you.

Your time horizon determines some kinds of risk. If you have a short time horizon, volatility is a larger risk than inflation. You should follow an asset allocation strategy that gives greater weight to principal stability. If you have a long time horizon, inflation is the more significant danger, and you should have larger allocations to equity investments. Regardless of the time horizon, however, broad diversification is a good idea for both conservative and aggressive investors.

There are uncertainties inherent in the process that cannot be avoided, and they often are difficult for investors to live with. It's natural to fear the unknown and to want to reduce or eliminate uncertainty whenever possible, but as past Federal Reserve Chairman Paul A. Volcker said, "You cannot hedge the world."

People want to believe that a professional can eliminate the uncertainties of investing. But that's not true. What is true is that focusing on the uncertainties inherent in money management provides nothing more than a better picture of the uncertainties. It will not eliminate them.

You may find this difficult to live with, but uncertainty is not necessarily bad. If you have a long time horizon, for example, short-run uncertainty is the engine that drives the higher returns of equity investing. If you can learn this lesson, you can use it to your advantage. There's a difference in understanding something intellectually and living with the results on a day-to-day basis. Successful investing is a psychological process as much as it is a money management—or money-making—endeavor.

Without a very firm commitment to long-term investment policies, it's easy for an investor to be distracted by schemes that promise high returns with little or no risk. If you depart from your long-term strategies to pursue these investments, you will end up building a portfolio the same way you collected shells at the beach as a child—by picking up whatever catches your eye at any given moment.

There is no safe, quick, or easy way to build wealth, and there are no guarantees. There are only tried-and-true methods and a few useful guidelines.

Imagine that you're standing in the middle of a large group of slot machines at a Las Vegas gambling casino. All around you, you hear the sound of people winning as the jackpots from lucky pulls of the handle drop coins noisily into the metal catcher. Now, while it's always true that at any point in time some people are ahead of the game, on average the flow of money is from the pockets of the gamblers to the offices of the casino that owns the machines. Objectively you know this, but in the midst of the magic of a casino, excitement can override better judgment as players win just often enough to make them believe they can get ahead by playing the game. Fueling their hope for beating this system is the evidence of their senses, which tell them that other people are indeed winning, and they can, too, if only they could find a hot machine.

The messages you receive from the day-to-day investment environment can be as distracting and misleading as the sounds of the intermittent winnings of slot machines. Whether it comes from a new market-timing guru or an investment idea that seems to promise better results than a well-diversified portfolio, there will always be temptations that encourage investors to depart from well-conceived long-term plans. My advice? Resist the temptation.

LET'S REMEMBER THIS:

- ► The time horizon is the most important element of any investment plan.

- ► Avoid investment distractions, like "get-rich-quick" schemes.

- ► Stay focused on your dreams and your financial plan.

▼

COMMON MISTAKES AND HOW TO REMEDY THEM

1. **Mistake:** Most investors do not know what to look for and consequently start off with undefined goals and bad investment selection criteria, which lead to poor stock selection.

    Remedy: Decide what your goals are. Create an investment plan, and use the techniques in Chapter 6 to choose your winning blue chip stocks.

2. **Mistake:** Many investors believe they can average down the price of the stocks they own by buying more shares as the prices drops, which is technically true. However, why is the stock price moving down and will it change course through time and for what reason?

    Remedy: Remember, you only make money when the stock price goes up.

3. **Mistake:** People tend to buy stocks selling at low prices per share. They think it's better to buy more shares of a lower-priced stock than fewer of a higher-priced stock.

    Remedy: The price is irrelevant. You must focus on investment dollars, not numbers of shares. Remember, stocks are like anything else; the higher the quality, the higher the price. That's not to say that a stock is of dubious quality simply because it sells for $5 to $10. However, the commission percentages are higher with respect to total dollars invested for lower priced stocks: Institutions do not buy them, they tend to be more volatile, and they therefore represent higher risk to your portfolio.

4. **Mistake:** Inexperienced investors want to make a killing. They're looking for the easy way to make a quick buck and get rich. Not making a plan, not thoroughly researching your investment choices, and not following through with your decisions, all of which are time consuming, will lead to disaster.

    Remedy: Remember, only through a disciplined approach and patient investing will you increase your odds of being successful financially.

5. **Mistake:** Investors love tips. Never buy on a tip or story or rumor. Often, tips are wrong; when tips are in error, the price of stock usually reacts negatively.

    Remedy: There is no substitute for sound investment practices. Eliminate market hype, emotion, and gut feelings—just stick to sound fundamentals.

6. **Mistake:** Most investors hold onto their losses and sell their profits.

    Remedy: This is exactly the opposite of what an astute investor should do. Let your profits run, sell losses, and always upgrade your portfolio.

7. **Mistake:** Most investors hesitate to buy stocks that are at or near their highs. To most investors, the price is simply too high. Your instincts may well lead you to the wrong conclusions; the market will not.

    Remedy: There is a reason why stocks are at their highs. Buy them and watch them go even higher.

8. **Mistake:** Investors often focus too heavily on taxes and commissions.

    Remedy: Your focus should be on making profits. When your focus is on taxes and commissions, you make inappropriate decisions based on tax sheltering, saving brokerage fees, or trying to qualify for long-term capital gains. Paying commissions is relatively minor when compared to making the correct investment decisions and taking the correct actions as markets dictate. The greatest advantages of owning common stocks is the relatively low commission costs, instant marketability, and liquidity versus real estate, where commissions are higher, liquidity is lower, and marketability is questionable.

9. **Mistake:** Investors tend to be influenced by things that are not particularly important over the long haul, such as stock splits, dividend changes, news announcements, and brokerage firm recommendations.

    Remedy: Stick with your plan and stay focused. To be successful, you must keep the distractions at bay.

▼

QUESTIONS & ANSWERS

1. What's the difference between a primary market for common stock and a secondary market?

The sale of new securities to raise funds is a primary market transaction. The proceeds of the sale of these securities represent new capital for the firm. New issues are typically underwritten by investment banking firms, which acquire the total issue from the company. They resell those securities in smaller units to individuals and institutional investors.

After the new issue of securities is sold in the primary market, subsequent trades of these securities take place in the secondary market. The secondary market is vital because it provides liquidity to investors who acquire securities in the primary market.

2. What's the relationship between NASDAQ and the OTC market?

The OTC market is the largest segment of the secondary market in terms of the numbers of securities (nearly 40,000). Although OTC stocks represent many small and unseasoned companies, the range of securities traded is very broad. This is a negotiated market where investors directly negotiate purchases and sales through dealers.

The NASDAQ system is a computerized system that provides current bid and ask prices on more than 5,000 of the most widely traded OTC securities. Through a dealer, a broker can instantly discover the bid and asked quotations offered by all dealers making a market in a stock. The broker can then contact the dealer offering the best price and negotiate a trade directly.

3. Why should an investor hold a diversified portfolio? What's the simplest way to diversify?

Diversification can substantially reduce the risk associated with investments. Diversity is simply not putting all your eggs in one basket. An effectively diversified portfolio reduces risk without cutting long-term average returns. In selecting blue chip stocks, investors should choose stocks whose risks are related to different economic, political, and social factors.

A diversified portfolio is very difficult to achieve when funds are limited. If you have limited funds, a mutual fund offers the opportunity to participate in an investment pool that can contain hundreds of different securities.

4. What is a growth stock?

A growth stock is a company whose earnings have significantly outstripped the earnings of other companies in the past and are expected to do so in the future. These companies tend to reinvest a large portion of their earnings and thus pay a relatively low (or no) dividend to shareholders. Investors who purchase these shares are more concerned with the appreciation in the market price of the stock than they are with the receipt of a cash dividend.

Because growth stocks provide little income, they depend on high growth rates to sustain a high stock price. If these growth rates fail to materialize, the stock price can fall dramatically. Consequently, investors in growth stocks should be aware of the greater risks that come with the possibility of earning the superior returns.

5. What's the difference between a bull market and a bear market? What are the implications of each to the investor?

A bull market is a prolonged rise in the price of stocks; a bear market is a prolonged decline in the price of stocks. Stock market movements are extremely important to investors. Historical studies indicate that 60% of stock price movements are directly related to movements in the overall market; 30% to 35% are related to sector or group movements; and only 5% are related to individual stock movements.

Because stock prices have generally risen over time, bull markets are predominant over bear markets. In fact, the market typically rises two out of every three years. Although bear markets tend to be substantially shorter than bull markets, the decline can be steep. Even including the crash of 1929, when stock prices plunged 89%, the average bear market loss has been about 36% from peak to trough.

6. Does a balance sheet disclose the current market value of assets?

Generally, no. Items reflected under property, plant, and equipment are shown at their original cost less total depreciation recognized on the asset (called *accumulated depreciation*). The current market value of these assets is not reflected in the financial statements. For many corporations, the amount shown for property, plant, and equipment on the balance sheet is but a small percentage of the current market value of the assets.

The balance sheet also fails to disclose certain assets of vital importance to the corporation. For example, the value of a corporation's human resources is not reflected in the balance sheet. Additionally, the value of brand names often is not disclosed, or if it is, it is shown at an unamortized cost, which has no relationship to its current market value. In recent years, the target of many takeovers has been to acquire valuable brand names.

7. How does the Securities and Exchange Commission serve the investor?

The Securities and Exchange Commission (SEC) was established by Congress to administer federal laws that seek to provide protection for investors. The overriding purpose of these laws is to ensure the integrity of the securities markets by requiring full disclosure of material facts related to securities offered for sale to the public.

The SEC does not insure investors. Nor does it prevent the sale of securities in risky, poorly managed, or unprofitable companies. Rather, registration with the SEC is designed to provide adequate and accurate disclosure of required material facts about the company and the securities it proposes to sell. A portion of the information included in the registration statement is included in a prospectus prepared for public distribution.

The SEC requires the continual disclosure of company activities through annual, quarterly, and special reports. Form 10-K is the annual report; it contains a myriad of financial data and non-financial information, such as the names of corporate officers and directors and the extent of their ownership.

Form 10-Q is the quarterly report; it contains abbreviated financial and non-financial information. Form 8-K is a report of material events or corporate changes deemed important to shareholders or the SEC. All of these reports can be obtained from the company or from the SEC.

▼

WHAT IS RISK [STANDARD DEVIATION]?

The *standard deviation* of a series is the extent to which observations in the series differ from the arithmetic mean. (The *arithmetic mean* is the simple average of the asset's returns.) It is a measure of the volatility, or risk, of the asset. The higher the standard deviation, the larger the dispersion of returns around the mean, thus, the larger the risk.

Investment risk is based on the notion of uncertainty. If it is less certain that the asset class will be near its expected return, then there is more uncertainty and risk contained in that asset class.

Statistically, risk is measured by standard deviation. Standard deviation is an estimate of the possible future dispersion (or divergence) of the actual returns to be generated by the asset class around its expected return. It measures the potential magnitude of any positive performance or negative performance of an asset class from its expected return.

STANDARD DEVIATION [RISK] CONCEPTS:

▶ **Expected Returns.** The expected return falls in the middle of the chart. Exactly 50% of the area is to the right of the expected return; the other 50% is to the left of the expected return.

▶ **One Standard Deviation.** About 68% of the area falls within the area marked on the graph. This represents one standard deviation below and above the expected return.

▶ **Two Standard Deviations.** About 96% of the area falls within all of the marked regions. This represents two standard deviations from the expected return.

In a normal distribution, about two-thirds of the observations fall within one standard deviation of the average return; and about 95% of the observations fall within two standard deviations. (A normal distribution is shaped like a bell curve.)

Figure C-1 shows the frequency distributions, or histograms, of historic annual returns for blue chip stocks and long-term government bonds. This graph vividly illustrates the differences between the two assets.

Figure C-1   Stock and Bond Price Distributions

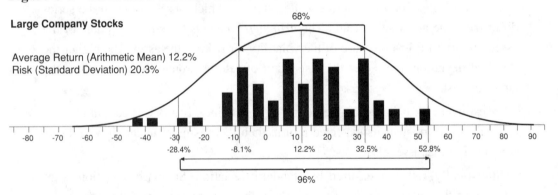

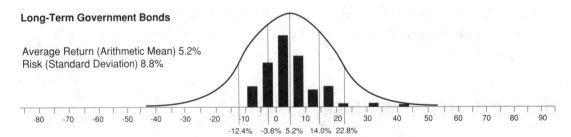

Riskier assets, such as stocks, have low, spread out histograms that reflect the broad distribution of returns from very low to very high. Historically, returns have been dispersed around a stock's average return of 12.2%. Based on a stock's standard deviation of 20.3%, roughly two-thirds of the annual returns should fall between −8.1% and 32.5%, and approximately 95% should fall between −28.5% and 52.8%.

The histogram for long-term bonds, a less risky asset, is much narrower, indicating fewer fluctuations of return. With an average return of 5.2% and a much lower standard deviation of 8.8%, approximately two-thirds of the long-term government bonds' past returns are between −3.6% and 14% and roughly 95% are between −12.4% and 22.8%.

What Is Correlation Coefficient?

If two asset classes are similarly influenced by factors that cause their prices to change, their return movements will be closely linked. As a consequence, the combination of these asset classes does not produce an asset mix with a standard deviation that is much lower than the average standard deviation of the component asset classes.

By combining asset classes that are influenced differently by the same factors that cause their prices to change, the standard deviation of the asset mix can be reduced significantly below the average standard deviation for the component asset classes. One asset class might tend to perform poorly at the same time that another asset class is doing well. When combined in a portfolio, each asset class will tend to offset the other's returns, thereby reducing the variability of returns in the entire portfolio.

The standard deviation of the asset mix partially depends on the extent of co-movement (or *co-variance*) of the asset class returns. The correlation coefficients measure the degree of association between the returns of two asset classes. Correlation coefficients range in value from –1.0 to +1.0.

Interpreting Correlation Coefficients

1. **Perfectly Positively Correlated.** A correlation coefficient of +1.0 implies that the returns between two asset classes move in lock-step with one another. This does not mean necessarily that they also move in equal increments.

If the returns for one asset class change two units for every one unit of change in the other asset class, the changes in returns differ by a factor of two, but they still have a correlation of +1.0.

The chart in Figure D-1 shows the relationship between two asset classes whose returns are perfectly positively correlated with one another and whose standard deviations are equal to each other.

Figure D-1   +1.0 Correlation Coefficient

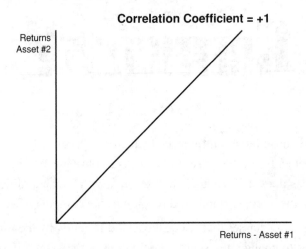

2. **Perfectly Negatively Correlated.** A correlation coefficient of –1.0 implies that the returns between two asset classes change inversely with one another in a perfect manner. When one asset class goes up, the other asset class moves down. Again, the absolute magnitude of changes may not necessarily be the same.

If the returns of one asset class change upward two units for every one downward unit change in the other asset class, the changes in returns differ in their increment, but they are negatively inversely correlated and have a correlation of –1.0.

The chart in Figure D-2 depicts the relationship between two asset classes whose returns are perfectly negatively correlated with one another and whose standard deviations are equal to each other.

Figure D-2   –1.0 Correlation Coefficient

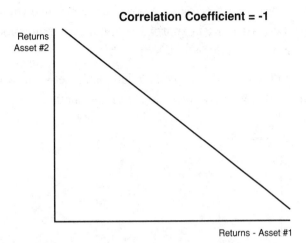

3. Uncorrelated. If the correlation coefficient equals 0, the returns between two asset classes are uncorrelated with one another. The movements of each asset class are approximately independent of each other. The chart in Figure D-3 shows the relationship between two asset classes whose returns are uncorrelated with one another.

Figure D-3   0 Correlation Coefficient

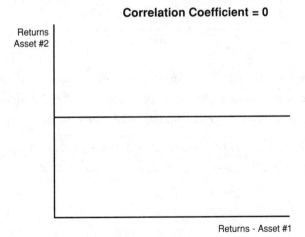

4. **Positively Correlated.** If the correlation coefficient is between 0 and +1, the returns between two asset classes are positively correlated with one another. The two asset classes move in approximately the same direction. However, they do not move perfectly in lock-step with one another.

   The chart in Figure D-4 depicts the relationship between two asset classes whose returns are positively correlated with one another.

Figure D-4   Positive Correlation

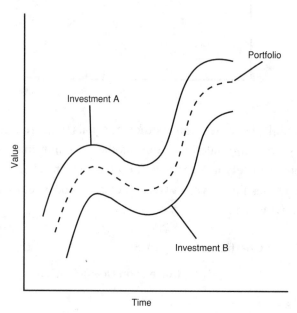

5. **Negatively Correlated.** If the correlation coefficient is between 0 and −1, the return between two asset classes is negatively correlated with one another. The two asset classes move in opposite directions from one another.

   The chart in Figure D-5 shows the relationship between two asset classes whose returns are negatively correlated with one another.

Figure D-5   Negative Correlation

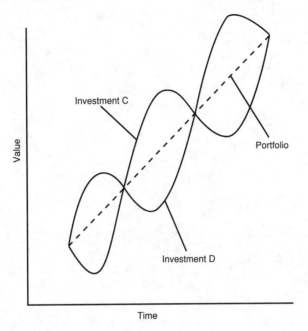

APPENDIX E

▼

THE MODEL PORTFOLIO

Figure E-1 The Model Portfolio

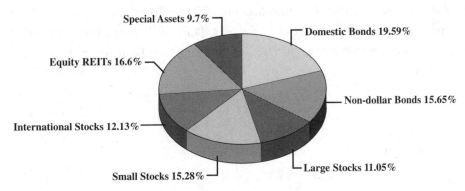

Table E-1 shows the optimum mix of the seven investment asset classes, providing the highest rate of returns with the lowest risk.

Table E-1 Optimum Portfolio Mix	
Asset Class	*% of Total*
Domestic bonds	20.33%
International bonds	16.31%
Blue chip stocks	10.86%
Small capitalization stocks	14.34%
International stocks	11.91%
Real estate	15.81%
Special assets	10.44%

continues

Table E-1   Optimum Portfolio Mix [Continued]

Asset Class	% of Total
Average rate of return	12.53%
Average variation (two standard deviations)	16.89%
Probability of losing purchasing power	
Over one-year period	7.35%
Over five-year period	0.68%

Historically, this asset mix has produced an average annual total return of 12.53%. The variation annually on that return has been plus or minus 16.89%.

If you take inflation (of 4%) into account, this portfolio has the possibility of losing purchasing power over any one year period of 7.35%; over a five-year period, which is a more reasonable time horizon for investing, that figure drops to .68%.

▼

The Efficient Frontier

The efficient frontier plays a central role in portfolio allocation. It is the means by which Modern Portfolio Theory is applied to the asset allocation decision.

Modern Portfolio Theory

Modern Portfolio Theory describes how asset classes can be combined into diversified asset mixes. In March 1952 Harry Markowitz published the landmark article titled "Portfolio Selection," in the *Journal of Finance,* which first described the efficient frontier. He was subsequently awarded the Nobel Prize in Economics for this concept.

Modern Portfolio Theory assumes that:

► Investors are rational and act to maximize the performance of their investments given their risk tolerance.

► Investors choose portfolios according to the expected return and risk characteristics.

► Rational investors prefer less risk and more return.

► Expected return is defined as the total return including income plus capital appreciation.

► Risk is defined as uncertainty. It is an estimate of the possible variability around the expected return. The statistical measure of risk that is commonly used is standard deviation.

Portfolio Optimization

An efficient portfolio is defined as a portfolio that has a maximum expected return for any level of risk or a minimum level of risk for any expected return.

Portfolio optimization is a mathematical technique for quickly identifying efficient portfolios. It takes into account the expected return and the risk (standard deviation) of each asset class, as well as the correlation of returns between different asset classes in the portfolio.

The important factor in gaining diversification in an asset mix is the correlation between the asset classes. The general mathematical technique of portfolio optimization is called *quadratic programming*. It is an iterative process that must be repeated many times for each level of portfolio risk to find the asset mix that provides the highest level of expected returns.

Efficient Frontier

A continuum of efficient asset mixes can be traced in dimensions of expected returns and risk to form what is called the *efficient frontier*. It is a line traced around the boundary that connects all the efficient portfolios. This line forms the efficient frontier. (A typical efficient frontier can be seen in Figure F-1.) According to Modern Portfolio Theory, rational investors would restrict their asset mix choices to those asset mixes that appear in the efficient frontier.

Figure F-1   Efficient Frontier Graph

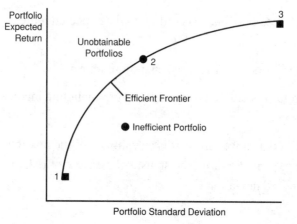

Maximum Return Asset Mix (Mix 3)

At the extreme right of the efficient frontier, this asset mix offers the highest portfolio expected return, but also requires the greatest amount of portfolio risk. This portfolio would be invested entirely in the asset class with the highest expected return. In a generic portfolio, this would typically be all stocks. A portfolio consisting entirely of the riskiest asset class will always fall on the efficient frontier as long as it also offers the highest expected return. This is because, although it is possible to reduce portfolio risk by combining this asset class with another asset class that is not perfectly positively correlated, the reduction in risk can only be accomplished at the expense of lowering portfolio expected return.

Minimum Risk Asset Mix (Mix 1)

At the extreme left on the efficient frontier, this asset mix offers a relatively low expected portfolio return, which is highly reliable because it also has a low portfolio risk. If the component asset class were stocks, bonds, and cash, this asset mix would typically be heavily weighted toward cash. However, the asset class having the lowest standard deviation will not lie on the efficient frontier unless it is perfectly positively correlated with the other asset classes or has no risk at all. Otherwise, it is possible to combine the minimum risk asset class with another asset class with which it is not perfectly positively correlated to create an asset mix that has a lower portfolio risk and a higher portfolio expected return.

Inefficient Asset Mixes

Asset mixes that are plotted below the efficient frontier are inefficient asset mixes. They are undesirable because it is possible to increase portfolio expected return without incurring additional portfolio risk (Mix 2). Alternately, the same level of portfolio expected return also could be preserved with lower portfolio risk.

Unobtainable Asset Mixes

Asset mixes above the efficient frontier would be preferred, but no such asset mixes exist based on the characteristics of the current asset classes. The efficient frontier can be regarded as a constraint. It represent the best possible combinations of portfolio expected return and portfolio risk available for consideration.

GLOSSARY

▼

Arbitage: Profiting from differences in price when the same security is traded on two or more markets.

Balance Sheet: The financial statement of a business or institution that lists the assets, debts, and owner's investment as of a specific date.

Bear: Person who believes that stock prices will drop.

Bear Market: An extended period of a downturn in the prices of securities. It does not necessarily mean that all prices of stocks or all industries fall.

Beta: A mathematical measure of the sensitivity of rates of return of a portfolio as compared with rates of return on the market as a whole. A high beta (over 1) indicates moderate or high price volatility. A beta of 1.5 forecasts a 1.5% change in the return on an asset for every 1% change in the return on the market. A beta of 1 means that the stock price will likely move with the market. No matter what the beta is, by itself it is not a reason to buy (or not buy) any stock.

Big Board: Trader's term for the New York Stock Exchange.

Blue Chip: A very high-quality investment involving a lower-than-average risk of loss of principal or reduction in income. The term generally refers to securities of companies having a long history of sustained earnings and dividend payments.

Book Value: Common shareholders' equity on a per-share basis. Calculated by subtracting liabilities from assets and dividing the remainder by the number of out-standing shares of stock. In other words, the book value is what the stock is worth regardless of its market price.

Bull: Person who believes that stock prices will rise.

Bull Market: An extended period of time when prices generally increase in value. It does not necessarily mean that all prices of stocks in all industries rise.

Business Cycle: The somewhat irregular, recurring periods of change in economic activity. It is usually divided into four stages: expansion, prosperity, contraction, and recession. Firms that experience large swings in sales and profits are most severely impacted by business cycles.

Call Option: The right of a buyer to purchase a specified quantity of a security interest at a fixed price at any time during the life of the option.

Callable: The option of a company to call in a security and redeem it for cash.

Chief Financial Officer (CFO): The person responsible to the company's board of directors for carrying out its financial policies.

Common Stock: A class of capital stock that has no preference to dividends or any distribution of assets. Common stockholders are the residual owners of a corporation in that they have a claim to what remains after every other party has been paid.

Conversion Price: The price per share at which common stock will be exchanged for a convertible security (a warrant or an option).

Convertible Security: Bond or share of preferred stock that can be exchanged into a specified amount of common stock at a specified price.

Corporation: A business that is granted a state charter, which recognizes it as a separate legal entity with its own rights, privileges, and liabilities distinct from those of the individuals forming the business. Shareholders are part-owners of corporations.

Current Assets: Cash, or an asset expected to be converted into cash within one year. Assets include cash, marketable securities, accounts receivables, inventories, and prepaid expenses. They tend to add liquidity and safety to a firm's operation.

Current Ratio: A measure of a firm's ability to meet its short-term obligations. It is calculated by dividing current liabilities into current assets. A high ratio usually indicates high liquidity as well as conservative and good management. A 5:1 or 6:1 ratio is excellent; 10:1 or 20:1 is even better. If you find a ratio of anything less than 1:1, that company has greater liabilities than assets and is therefore not viable as an addition to your portfolio.

Cyclical Stock: Common stock of a firm whose profits are heavily influenced by cyclical changes in general economic activity.

Deficit: A negative retained-earnings balance. A deficit is the result of a company's accumulated losses and dividend payments exceeding earnings.

Discount Rate: Rate of interest charged by the Federal Reserve to member banks.

Discretionary Account: A brokerage account in which the customer permits the broker to act on the customer's behalf when buying and selling securities. The broker has discretion as to the choice of securities, prices, and timing, subject to any limitations specified in the agreement. Because of their riskiness, discretionary accounts should be avoided.

Diversification: The acquisition of a group of assets in which returns on the assets are not directly related over time. Proper investment diversification, requiring a sufficient number of different assets, reduces the risk in particular securities.

Dividends: Payments made by a corporation to its stockholders.

Earnings: Income of a business; the term usually refers to after-tax income.

Earnings Per Share (EPS): Net income for a given period divided by the average number of common shares outstanding during that period.

Economic Growth: Increased production levels of goods and services.

Emerging Growth Stock: The common stock of a relatively young firm operating in an industry with very good growth prospects. Although such stock offers unusually large returns, it could be risky if the expected growth does not occur.

Federal Reserve Board: Seven members of the Federal Reserve who oversee the formulation of monetary policy and control of the money supply.

Financial Leverage: Accelerative effect of debt on financial returns.

Financial Ratios: Indicators of a company's financial performance and position.

Financial Risk: The risk that a firm will be unable to meet its financial obligations. This is primarily a function of the relative amount of debt that the firm uses to finance its assets.

Fundamental Analysis: Process of estimating a security's value by analyzing the basic financial and economic facts about the company that issues the security.

Golden Parachute: Lucrative compensation packages guaranteed to executives in the event of a takeover. (Mergers, buyouts, etc., are included as well.)

Greenmail: Purchase by a corporation of its own stock from a potential acquirer at a price substantially greater than the market price. In exchange, the acquirer agrees to drop the takeover bid.

Growth Stock: The stock of a firm that is expected to have above-average increases in revenues and earnings. These firms normally retain most earnings for reinvestment and therefore pay a small dividend, if any.

Hedge Against Inflation: An investment whose growth outpaces inflation.

Hedging: Actions taken by investors to reduce a possible loss.

Incentive Stock Option: An option permitting an employee to purchase shares of the employer's stock at a predetermined price.

Income Statement: Financial statement showing a firm's revenues and expenses over a prescribed period of time.

Inflation: A general increase in the price of goods and services. Unexpected inflation tends to be detrimental to security prices primarily because it forces interest rates higher.

Interest Rate Risk: The risk that interest rates will rise and reduce the market value of an investment and the value of stocks. Long-term fixed income securities, such as bonds and preferred stock, subject their owners to the greatest amount of interest rate risk. Short-term instruments are influenced less by interest rate movements.

Intrinsic Value: The value of a security, such as a warrant. The price of a stock less the conversion price of the warrant equals the intrinsic value of the warrant.

Investment Advisor: A person who offers professional investment advice for a fee.

Investment Banking: Industry that specializes in assisting business firms and governments in marketing new securities.

Junk Bond: A high-risk, high-yield bond with less than an S&P rating of BBB. (S&P rates bonds according to various risk factors and gives them an AAA for the strongest, AA for the next strongest, A, then BBB and so forth, to D, which is the lowest rating, meaning the bond is in default.) It is generally issued by either a new company or by an established company to fund a corporate takeover.

Leverage: The ability to control something larger with something smaller. Leverage is utilized as an attempt to get more bang for your buck.

Leverage Buy Out: Process of buying a corporation's stock with borrowed money, then repaying at least part of the debt from the corporation's assets.

Liquidity: When a large portion of one's holdings are in cash or in assets that can be converted into cash quickly.

Load Fund: Type of mutual fund where the buyer must pay a sales fee or commission on top of the price.

Loss of Purchasing Power: When inflation rates increase faster than wages, earnings, and the values of investments.

Managed Account: An investment account managed by a broker or other professional. Managed accounts are designed for investors who lack the time or expertise to make their own decisions.

Margin Account: A brokerage account that permits an investor to purchase securities by borrowing the cash value out of securities already held in an account. Usually they offer a lower interest rate on the loan as well as tax deductions on the interest paid. A margin account gives you leverage and, in good markets, can enhance your returns; the risk is that in bad markets you could lose most or all of your money.

Margin Risk: The risk that general market pressures will cause the value of an investment to fluctuate. It may be necessary to liquidate a position (sell) during a down period in the cycle. Market risk is highest for securities with above-average volatility (such as common stock), and lowest for stable securities (such as Treasury bills). Market risk is of little consequence to a person who purchases securities with the intention of holding them for a long period of time.

Margin Trading: Using borrowed funds for trading; also known as trading on credit. Margin trading is governed by Federal Reserve and stock exchange regulations.

Market Efficiency: Description of how prices in competitive markets react to new information.

Merger: Combination of two or more firms into one.

Monetary Policy: Actions outlined by the Federal Reserve to control the money supply, bank lending, and interest rates.

NASDAQ (National Association of Securities Dealers Automated Quotations): A computerized communications network that provides quotations (bid and asked prices) on stock.

Net Income: Income after all expenses and taxes have been deducted. It's used to calculate various profitability and stock performance measures including price/earnings ratio, return on equity, and earnings per share.

No-load Fund: One type of mutual fund for which no commission is charged to make a purchase.

OTC Market (Over-the-counter market): In this market investors trade securities through a centralized computer telephone network that links dealers across the U.S.

Poison Pill: Tactic used by corporations to defend against unfriendly takeovers, generally by making a takeover more expensive.

Portfolio: An investor's collection of securities.

Price/Earnings Ratio: The current price of a stock divided by the current earnings per share of the issuing firm. As a rule, a relatively high P/E ratio is an indication that the firm's earnings are likely to grow or the stock price is likely to fall.

Prospectus: Formal written offer to sell securities, including audited financial statements and other information about the company.

Put Option: Right of a buyer to sell a specified quantity of a security interest at a fixed price anytime during the life of the option.

Recession: An extended decline in general business activity. Usually defined by three consecutive quarters of falling gross domestic product.

Registration Statement: Contains a firm's financial statements and other information. This is filed with the Securities and Exchange Commission each time a new security is offered to the public.

Revenue: The inflow of assets resulting from the sale of goods and services as well as earnings from dividends, interest, and rent. It is usually received either as cash or as receivables that can be turned into cash at a later date (also referred to as *sales* of a company).

Reverse Stock Split: A proportionate decrease in the shares of stock held by stockholders. For example, a 1-for-3 split results in the stockholder owning one share for every three shares owned before the split. A company usually institutes a reverse split to increase the market price of the stock by decreasing the number of shares outstanding. See *stock split*, which is the opposite.

Risk: The variability of returns from an investment; the greater the variability, the greater the risk.

Secondary Offering: Public sale of previously issued securities owned by large investors.

Short Sale: Sale of a borrowed security with the intention of purchasing it later at a lower price.

Short Term: Designating a gain or loss on the value of an asset that has been held less than a specified period of time.

Special Situation: A currently undervalued stock that can suddenly increase in value because of potentially favorable circumstances. Special situations are quite risky.

Statement of Cash Flows: Financial statement showing a firm's cash receipts and cash payments over a period of time.

Stock Dividend: Pro rata distribution of additional shares of stock to stockholders.

Stock Market Averages: Average of the market prices of a specified number of stocks.

Stock Split: When a corporation reduces the market price of its stock (by splitting its stock) to make the shares more attractive to investors. The share price is reduced proportionally with the percentage of increased outstanding shares.

Stock Table: Summary of the trading activity of individual securities.

Technical Analysis: Process of predicting future stock price movements by analyzing the historical movement of stock prices and the supply and demand forces that affect those prices.

Tender Offer: Offer by one firm to the stockholders of another firm to purchase a specified number of shares at a specified price within a specified time period.

Uptick Trade: Transactions executed at a price higher than the previous trade.

White Knight: Person or corporation who saves a corporation from a hostile takeover by taking it over on more favorable terms.

Yield: The percentage return on an investment. For example, if a stock is selling at a price of $30 and pays a $1 dividend, then the stock yields 3.3% ($1 divided by its stock price of $30). There are many types of yields but the preceding example is used only for illustrative purposes in this book.

BIBLIOGRAPHY

▼

Buchsbaum, William M., *The Little Book of Big Profits.* Macmillan USA, 1996.

Case, Samuel, *Big Profits from Small Stocks.* Prime Publishing, 1994.

Dent, Jr., Harry S., *The Great Boom Ahead.* Hyperion, 1993.

Edwards, Samuel P., *Remember the Vine: How to Grow Rich and Stay Rich.* Beacon Investment Company, 1990.

Ellis, Charles D., *Investment Policy: How to Win the Loser's Game.* Business One Irwin, 1993.

O'Higgins, Michael, *Beating the Dow.* HarperCollins Publishers, 1991.

O'Neil, William J., *How to Make Money in Stocks: A Winning System in Good Times and Bad.* McGraw–Hill, Inc., 1995.

INDEX

▼

A

B

Histograms, 138–39
Hulbert Guide to Financial
  Newsletters, 58
Hulbert, Mark, 58

I

Ibbotson, Roger, 30
Imports, 87, 88
Incentive stock option, 155
Income statement, 156
Index investing, 115
Individual Retirement Accounts
  (IRAs), 65
Industrial index. *See* Standard &
  Poor's 400 Index
Inefficient asset mixes, 151
Inflation, 1, 12–14, 95, 127
  defined, 12, 156
  hedge against, 33, 47, 128, 155
  history of, 7–8, 13, 20–21, 30
  measuring, 13
  purchasing power affected by, 12,
    13–14
Information resources, 57–61
Insider, The (newsletter), 59
Institutional holdings, 43
Interest rate risk, defined, 156
Interest rates, 96
  bond prices and, 104
  Keynesian Theory and, 120
  Monetarist Theory and, 120
  utility stocks and, 100, 103–5
International bonds, 123, 124, 147
International stocks, 123, 124, 147
International trade, 88–90
Internet information resources, 60
Intrinsic value, 121, 156

Investext, 60
Investing, 1–2
  changes in, xv–xvi
  defined, 1
  entails risk, 1, 11
  as a habit, 5–6, 8, 9
  as hobby, xv
  index, 115
  long-term. *See* Long-term investing
  passive, 115
  philosophies, 116–18
  short-term. *See* Short-term
    investing
  smart, xv–xvi
  special situation, 81–82, 84, 158
  structure for, 47–50
  uncertainties of, 128
Investment advisor, 156
Investment banking, 156
Investment goals, xv, 2–3, 8, 131
Investment newsletters, 58–59
Investment plans, 3–9
  building, 4–5
  diversification and, 19–23
  investing habit, 4–5, 8, 9
  as long-term, 6–8
  monthly check to, 5
  questions to ask, 4
  time horizon for, 8–9
Investment professionals, 112–14
Investor's Business Daily, 59, 94
Iraq, 73, 74

J

Japan, 75, 86, 90, 91
Joint ventures, international, 88–89
Junk bonds, 156

K

Keynes, John Maynard, 120
Keynesian Theory, 120

L

Labor, Bureau of, 77
Labor Statistics, Bureau of, 13
Large company stocks, 30–31
Leverage, 63, 156
Leverage buy out, 156
Liquidity, 113, 114
  defined, 156
Loaded funds, 114, 156
Long-term debt, 36, 44, 50
Long-term investing, 6–8, 113, 116, 128
  volatility and, 14–16
Loss of purchasing power, 12, 156

M

Magazines, 59
Malkiel, Burton, 115
Managed account, 156
Margin account, 63, 64–67, 156–57
  maintenance requirements, 64–65
  opening, 63
Margin agreement, 63
Margin risk, defined, 157
Margin trading, 63–67
  availability of funds, 65
  benefits of, 65–66
  commission expenses, 66–67
  defined, 157
  disadvantages of, 66–67
  interest expense, 66

margin loan rates, 65
rules governing, 64
Market action, 49, 50–55
Market efficiency, defined, 157
Market forecasting
  common solutions to, 106–7
  contrarian theory, 109–10
  Dow Theory, 97–100
  General Motors Bellwether
    Indicator, 101–3
  market timing, 110–12, 125
  news and the market, 105–6
  utility stocks and, 103–5
Markets, 26–30. *See also specific markets*
Market share, drop in, 70
Market timing, 110–12, 125
  information versus, 27
  limitations to, 111
  time versus, 6
Markowitz, Harry, 149
Maximum return asset mix, 151
Mergers, 71, 157
Merrill Lynch, 101
Metals, 123, 124
Minimum risk asset mix, 151
Mobil, 79, 80
Modern portfolio theory, 121–23, 147–51
Monetarist Theory, 120
Monetary policy, 157
Money Magazine, 59
Money managers, 112–14
Money market index, 20–21
Money supply, Monetarist Theory and, 120
Mutual funds, 114
  average annual returns on, 7
  diversification and, 134